D0403903

2/1
Game Force

Audrey Grant
and Eric Rodwell

BARON BARCLAY
BRIDGE SUPPLY

Published by
Baron Barclay

2/1 Game Force

Contact the author, see page 245.

Baron Barclay
3600 Chamberlain Lane, Suite 206
Louisville, KY 40241
U.S. and Canada: 1-800-274-2221
Worldwide: 502-426-0410
FAX: 502-426-2044
www.baronbarclay.com

ISBN-10: 0-939460-84-X
ISBN-13: 978-0-939460-84-7

Illustrations by Kelvin Smith
Design and composition by John Reinhardt Book Design

Printed in Canada

Contents

Contents

Acknowledgments

David Lindop is responsible for the structure and organization of all the material in the Audrey Grant Better Bridge series.

His experience as a Business Systems Architect, and background in the top levels of bridge, have provided the combination to ensure the material is carefully prepared, with each book enhancing the series.

David is a frequent competitor in international events. He is a three-time winner of the Canadian national championships. As an organizer, he holds the record of chairing the second largest bridge tournament in the world, attracting more than 22,000 tables in play.

David is an integral part of all the Audrey Grant projects, and is essential to their success.

Introduction

OVER THE DECADES, the experts have adjusted and improved their bidding systems. At one time, the fashion was to open four-card major suits; most players today open five-card majors. It used to be that any bid at the two level was strong and forcing. Now players like the advantages of weak two-bids. Change offers an opportunity to improve all aspects of our game. The key is to find material that is accurate and carefully organized, so that we feel enthusiastic and confident about trying new ideas. This book does just that. It introduces the basics of Two-Over-One Game Force, includes additional information for the curious, and sends the reader off eager to implement the latest inspirations of the experts.

Two-Over-One Game Force is simply an adaptation of Standard American bidding. It is not a new bidding system. It's now considered mainstream by most players. So even if we decide not to incorporate the ideas into our bidding system, it's an advantage to be comfortable with the opponents' auctions.

The goal of this book is to share the techniques and wisdom of the champions in a way that is comfortable and understandable to players with a wide range of experience and skill. Two-Over-One became popular because it can simplify, rather than complicate, the auction. Making one change to standard methods enables us to get to the best game contract and explore for slam with much more ease.

The structure of the book aims to respect the readers' time and energy. First, the information is on topic, carefully organized, and complete with summaries, exercises and sample deals illustrating the ideas. Finally, there are sixteen additional deals designed to review and consolidate the concepts in the book.

Since Two-Over-One Game Force is basically a change in the bidding messages, color-coding is used so the reader can recognize, at a glance, whether a bid is invitational, forcing, marathon, or a signoff.

Finally, we're proud of the quality of our team and the resources we have used to bring you the best information the world has to offer.

All the best,
Audrey Grant and Eric Rodwell

Two-Over-One fever seems to be sweeping organized bridge. Nearly every day, converts to the system look for more sources of information about how to play using this approach.

—MAX HARDY, Two Over One Game Force Quiz Book (1993)

Introduction to
Two-Over-One Game Force

Two-over-one Game Force (2/1) is not a new bidding system. It is simply a modification to standard bidding methods. It is designed to give the partnership more bidding room both to find the best game contract and explore slam possibilities. 2/1 is used when the opening bid is one-of-a-suit and the first response is a new suit at the two level.

When 2/1 Applies

Two-over-one Game Force applies only under certain conditions:

2/1 APPLIES WHEN:

- Opener bids 1♦, 1♥, or 1♠.
- The next player passes.
- Responder bids a new suit at the two level **without jumping**.
- Responder is an unpassed hand.

Here is an example of a 2/1 auction:

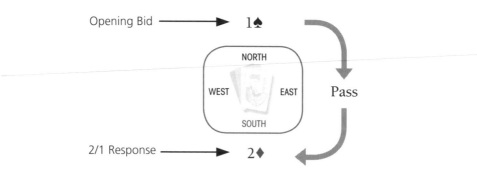

Opening Bid ⟶ 1♠

Pass

NORTH

WEST   EAST

SOUTH

2/1 Response ⟶ 2♦

There are only six auctions in which 2/1 applies, as shown on the following chart:

Opening Bid	2/1 Game Forcing Responses	
1♠	2♣, 2♦, 2♥	
1♥	2♣, 2♦	(2♠ skips a level)
1♦	2♣	(2♥/2♠ skip a level)
1♣	None	(2♦/2♥/2♠ skip a level)

Notice that 2/1 doesn't apply when the opening bid is 1♣ since responder can bid diamonds, hearts, or spades at the one level. Bidding a new suit at the two level would require a jump.

The Bidding Messages

The key to 2/1 Game Force is a change to the bidding message sent by the 2/1 response. So let's start with a review of the bidding messages. Every bid made during the bidding conversation sends a message to partner. It's important to have the message understood. Each bid carries one of four possible meanings:

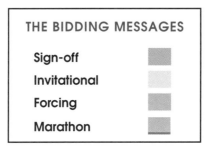

THE BIDDING MESSAGES

Sign-off

Invitational

Forcing

Marathon

Sign-off Bids

North opens with an invitational 1NT, showing a balanced hand of 15–17 points, and South raises to 3NT:

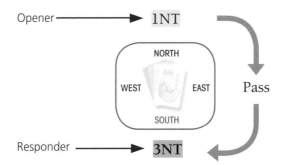

Opener ———————➤ 1NT

NORTH

WEST   EAST   Pass

SOUTH

Responder ————➤ 3NT

South has decided How High the partnership belongs, game. South has also decided Where the partnership belongs, notrump. Opener is expected to respect responder's decision and Pass.

Invitational Bids

North opens with an invitational 1♥ bid, and South raises to 2♥:

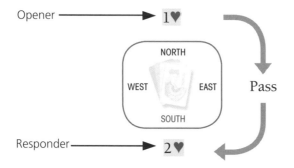

After an invitational response, opener may pass or bid again with the values to warrant improving the contract or moving toward game. With minimum values, North will pass the invitation; with a maximum, North can jump to game; with something in-between, North can make a further invitational bid, moving toward game.

Forcing Bids

North opens with an invitational 1♦ bid, and South responds 1♠:

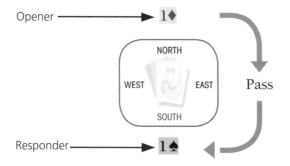

A new suit response at the one level is forcing, and opener must make a further descriptive bid. South's hand is unlimited in strength, so the partnership could belong in game, or even slam.

Marathon Bids

A forcing bid tells partner to bid again, but it doesn't commit the partnership to game. Partner won't have to keep bidding unless another forcing bid is made. This could make the auction awkward, since the partnership must continually be concerned about the bidding message of each call.

To simplify the subsequent auction, some bids are forcing to at least game. Both players must continue to bid until the game level is reached. These are referred to as *marathon bids*[1]. After a marathon bid, **How High** has been determined, to at least game. A marathon bid allows the partnership to find the best game, or to explore the possibility of a slam, without fear of the auction stopping too soon.

For example, suppose opener bids 1♥, responder bids 1♠, and opener jumps to 3♣:

Opener's *jump shift* to 3♣ is a marathon bid. Even with a minimum for the 1♠ bid, responder is expected to bid again, and neither partner can pass until a game contract is reached.

How does the partnership know whether a bid is sign-off, invitational, forcing, or marathon? It must decide on its agreements before the game begins. In many cases, intuition guides the partnership, and after a while, a pattern starts to emerge. The power of agreeing to play Two-over-one Game Force, however, is that it makes the bidding messages crystal clear in some key situations: when the partnership is looking for the best game or a possible slam.

---

[1] The term 'marathon bid' was introduced by Eric Rodwell in the *Joy of Bridge* (1984).

Two-Over-One Game Force

In standard methods, a 2/1 response is forcing for one round and promises about 10 or more points. The partnership can stop in a partscore contract if responder has fewer than 13 points and opener has a minimum opening. In the 2/1 Game-Forcing approach, a 2/1 response is a marathon bid, forcing to at least game.

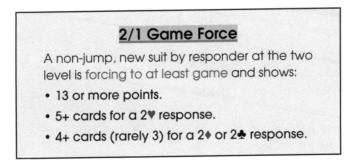

2/1 Game Force

A non-jump, new suit by responder at the two level is forcing to at least game and shows:

- 13 or more points.
- 5+ cards for a 2♥ response.
- 4+ cards (rarely 3) for a 2♦ or 2♣ response.

Here are examples of 2/1 Game Force responses:

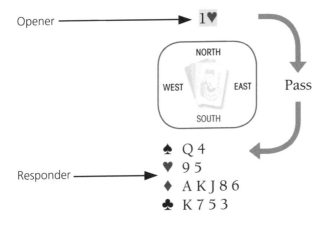

Opener ⟶ 1♥

Pass

```
        NORTH
WEST            EAST
        SOUTH
```

Responder ⟶
♠ Q 4
♥ 9 5
♦ A K J 8 6
♣ K 7 5 3

Respond 2♦. A new suit by responder at the two level, without a jump, starts the 2/1 Game Force auction. South's hand is worth 14 points—13 *high-card points* plus 1 *length point* for the five-card diamond suit, enough to commit the partnership to at least game.

This is the same response that would be made using standard methods. The difference is in the bidding message and the strength requirements. Playing 2/1 Game Force, South's 2♦ response is forcing to game and promises at least 13 points. In standard methods, the 2♦ response is only forcing for one round and could be made with as few as 10 points. After hearing opener's rebid, responder would have to show the extra strength to make sure the partnership gets to game.

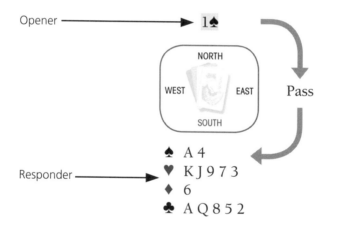

Opener ────────────► 1♠

NORTH

WEST   EAST   Pass

SOUTH

♠ A 4
Responder ────────────► ♥ K J 9 7 3
♦ 6
♣ A Q 8 5 2

Respond 2♥. After an opening bid of 1♠, a response of 2♥ shows a five-card or longer suit, as in standard methods. With two five-card suits, clubs and hearts, bid the higher-ranking suit, hearts, first. Playing 2/1 Game Force, the 2♥ response is forcing to at least game. In standard methods, the partnership is not yet committed to game.

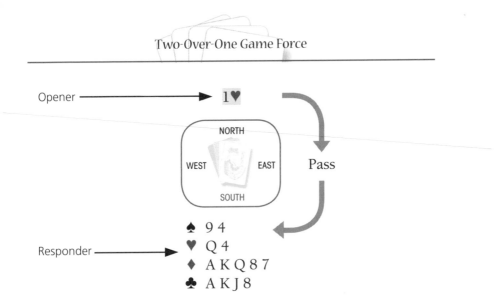

Respond 2♦. South has 19 high-card points plus 1 length point for a total of 20. In standard methods, South might make a *strong jump shift* to 3♦ to show the great strength and slam interest[2]. Playing 2/1 Game Force, there's no need to use up bidding space with a jump shift in this situation. The 2♦ response is forcing to game, leaving plenty of room to explore for slam along the way.

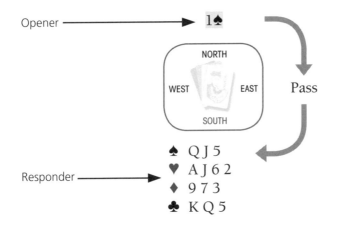

Respond 2♣. South has 13 high-card points, enough for a 2/1 Game Forcing response. With only three spades, South can't make

---

[2] In general, responder should avoid making a jump shift with a two-suited hand. It takes up a lot of bidding room, making it difficult to describe the distribution of the hand.

an immediate forcing raise, and 2♥ would promise a five-card suit. Occasionally, responder's only option is to bid a three-card minor. North will probably expect a longer club suit, but South is always planning to play with spades as trumps. 2♣ is just a *temporizing* bid.

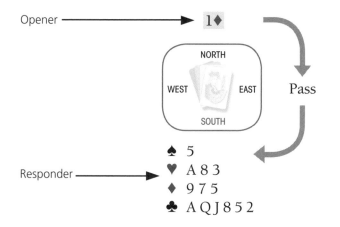

Opener ⟶ 1♦

NORTH

WEST   EAST   Pass

SOUTH

♠ 5
Responder ⟶ ♥ A 8 3
♦ 9 7 5
♣ A Q J 8 5 2

Respond 2♣. 2♣ is the only 2/1 Game Force responder can make after a 1♦ opening bid. South has 11 high-card points plus 2 length points for the six-card suit, enough to commit the partnership to game after North opens the bidding. The auction would start the same way in standard methods, but the 2♣ response would be forcing one round only, not to game.

Advantages of 2/1 Game Force

When responder's first bid establishes that the partnership is going to at least a game contract, all bids after the 2/1 response are forcing until the goal is reached. The auction can proceed comfortably, and the partnership can explore the best place to play game, or the possibility of a slam, without fearing that the auction will be passed out before game is reached. A good way to see the impact of 2/1 Game Force is to compare auctions using standard methods with those using 2/1.

THE PARTNERSHIP FINDS THE BEST GAME

Consider the following partnership hands:

OPENER	RESPONDER
♠ K J 7 5 3	♠ Q 2
♥ A K 9 7 2	♥ Q 8 3
♦ 8 4	♦ A J 3
♣ 6	♣ A 10 9 5 4

Using standard methods, the auction would begin:

OPENER	RESPONDER
1♠	2♣
2♥	?

After the 1♠ opening bid, showing 13 or more points, responder, with 13 high-card points plus 1 length point for the five-card club suit, knows How High: the partnership belongs in at least game. Responder doesn't yet know Where the contract belongs and starts with a forcing response of 2♣. After opener shows the second suit, responder is still unsure about the best spot. Opener might have only four hearts, so responder doesn't want to jump to 4♥.

This is where the standard auction becomes fuzzy. Responder has two choices: to jump to game; or to make a forcing bid, such as the bid of a new suit. Responder would probably jump to 3NT[3]. Now opener is faced with a dilemma. To show the fifth heart, opener could bid 4♥, but responder might have only one or two hearts and 3NT could be the best spot. Opener is unsure whether to bid again or to pass 3NT.

Playing 2/1 Game Force, the auction would be a lot crisper:

OPENER	RESPONDER
♠ K J 7 5 3	♠ Q 2
♥ A K 9 7 2	♥ Q 8 3
♦ 8 4	♦ A J 3
♣ 6	♣ A 10 9 5 4

OPENER	RESPONDER
1♠	2♣
2♥	2NT
3♥	4♥
PASS	

Responder's 2♣ is a marathon bid, forcing to at least game. Opener's 2♥ bid is also forcing to game. Responder can bide time by bidding only 2NT because it is still forcing. This gives opener the opportunity to rebid the heart suit comfortably at the three level. Now responder has all the information needed to choose the best contract. Opener doesn't have the extra strength needed to consider slam and passes.

---

[3] A discussion of the pros and cons of using fourth suit forcing in this type of situation can be found in Appendix 1.

Let's change opener's hand slightly:

OPENER	RESPONDER
♠ K J 10 7 5 3	♠ Q 2
♥ A K 7 2	♥ Q 8 3
♦ 8 4	♦ A J 3
♣ 6	♣ A 10 9 5 4

Playing standard methods, the auction would again start:

OPENER	RESPONDER
1♠	2♣
2♥	?

If responder were to jump to 4♥, the partnership would miss the spade fit and land in a precarious 4-3 heart fit. If responder were to jump to 3NT, opener would be unsure whether to bid 4♠; responder could have a singleton or void in spades.

Using 2/1 Game Force, the auction would go very smoothly:

OPENER	RESPONDER
♠ K J 10 7 5 3	♠ Q 2
♥ A K 7 2	♥ Q 8 3
♦ 8 4	♦ A J 3
♣ 6	♣ A 10 9 5 4

OPENER	RESPONDER
1♠	2♣
2♥	2NT
3♠	4♠
PASS	

Since responder's 2NT bid is still forcing, opener can complete the description of the hand pattern by rebidding the spades, showing six spades and four hearts. Responder has an easy time choosing WHERE the partnership belongs. Neither opener nor responder has the extra values to consider moving toward slam.

Let's change opener's hand once more:

OPENER	RESPONDER
♠ K J 7 5 3	♠ Q 2
♥ A K 7 2	♥ Q 8 3
♦ 8 4	♦ A J 3
♣ K 6	♣ A 10 9 5 4

Playing standard methods, the auction would likely go:

OPENER	RESPONDER
1♠	2♣
2♥	3NT
PASS	

Responder's jump to 3NT would put the partnership in its best spot.

However, using 2/1 Game Force, the auction would go equally smoothly:

OPENER	RESPONDER
1♠	2♣
2♥	2NT
3NT	PASS

Over responder's forcing 2NT bid, opener has nothing further to describe and simply raises to 3NT. Once again, the partnership has found a good contract after a 2/1 start.

2/1 Game Force can provide a relaxed way for the partnership to find WHERE it belongs, since both players know right away that they are headed for at least a game contract. There's no concern that the auction might suddenly stop in partscore. The partnership can focus on WHERE to play the contract, and both partners can comfortably describe their distribution.

THE PARTNERSHIP EXPLORES SLAM POSSIBILITIES

2/1 Game Force leaves more room for the partnership to consider the possibility of slam. Both partners have the opportunity to show extra strength and interest in slam without getting the partnership too high when there is a critical weakness in one of the suits. The partnership can exchange information about the *controls* that are important when considering a slam[4]—aces, kings, singletons, and voids. Blackwood is useful for slam bidding only when it is already clear that there is enough combined strength for slam and the only question is whether the partnership holds the appropriate number of aces and kings.

Consider these partnership hands:

OPENER	RESPONDER
♠ K J 9 7 5 2	♠ A Q 10
♥ A 4	♥ K Q 8 7 3
♦ 7 5 2	♦ A 6
♣ A 3	♣ J 6 4

Using standard methods, the auction is likely to go:

OPENER	RESPONDER
1♠	2♥
2♠	4♠

Responder has some interest in slam but there is no straightforward way to show the extra values. A raise to 3♠ would be invitational, not forcing. So responder will probably settle for a game contract.

---

[4] Showing controls is often referred to as *cuebidding*, but that term can be confusing since it is also used in competitive auctions when bidding a suit already bid by the opponents.

A jump to 4NT Blackwood, asking for aces, risks getting the partnership too high, since these might be the combined hands:

OPENER	RESPONDER
♠ K J 9 7 5 2	♠ A Q 10
♥ A 4	♥ K Q 8 7 3
♦ K J	♦ A 6
♣ 7 5 2	♣ J 6 4

The defenders could take the first three clubs tricks.

Responder would like a way to investigate the possibility of slam without getting the partnership overboard if it doesn't have controls in all the suits.

Playing 2/1, the partnership can comfortably explore for slam:

OPENER	RESPONDER
♠ K J 9 7 5 2	♠ A Q 10
♥ A 4	♥ K Q 8 7 3
♦ 7 5 2	♦ A 6
♣ A 3	♣ J 6 4

OPENER	RESPONDER	
1♠	2♥	
2♠	3♠	◄──── The Key Bid
4♣	4♦	
4♥	4NT	
5♥	5NT	
6♦	6♠	

After opener rebids 2♠, responder can afford to show the fit without using up space by jumping to game. Responder's 3♠ bid is forcing, since game has not yet been reached. Once spades have been agreed upon, opener can make a *control-showing* bid of 4♣ with the ♣A. Similarly, responder can show the control in diamonds by bidding 4♦. Opener can cooperate further by showing the heart control with 4♥. This is enough to convince responder to bid Blackwood, asking about aces and then kings, hoping for a grand slam. When opener shows only one king, responder settles for 6♠.

What if opener didn't have the ♣A?

OPENER	RESPONDER
♠ K J 9 7 5 2	♠ A Q 10
♥ A 4	♥ K Q 8 7 3
♦ K J	♦ A 6
♣ 7 5 2	♣ J 6 4

OPENER	RESPONDER	
1♠	2♥	
2♠	3♠ ←	The Key Bid
4♥	4♠	

When opener shows the ♥A but skips over showing a control in the club suit, responder decides to settle for game, and the partnership avoids getting too high. Responder's 4♠ call is not a signoff. Opener could bid again with extra values.

Slam bidding can be complex and is discussed further in Chapter 4, but it's easy to see how the extra room provided by the 2/1 game-forcing response can be critical in slam exploration.

When 2/1 Game Force is Off

Even if the partnership has agreed to play 2/1 as game forcing, there are two situations when it doesn't apply:

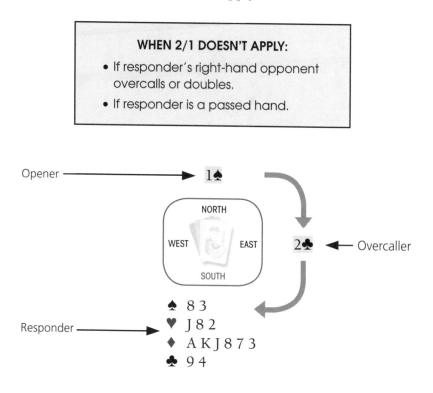

WHEN 2/1 DOESN'T APPLY:

• If responder's right-hand opponent overcalls or doubles.

• If responder is a passed hand.

Opener — 1♠

NORTH

WEST   EAST

2♣ — Overcaller

SOUTH

♠ 8 3
Responder — ♥ J 8 2
♦ A K J 8 7 3
♣ 9 4

Respond 2♦. After East's 2♣ overcall, South's bid of a new suit at the two level is still forcing—as in standard methods—but it is not forcing to game. In a competitive auction, it would be impractical for South to have to pass with this type of hand just because there are only 11 total points, not enough to force to game.

If South were to pass and West jumped to 3NT, for example, it's too late for South to show the diamond suit, and North might get off to a poor opening lead. South can afford to bid 2♦, promising 10 or more points, and then pass a 2♠ or 2NT rebid by North. If North now bids 2♥, South can rebid 3♦, non-forcing.

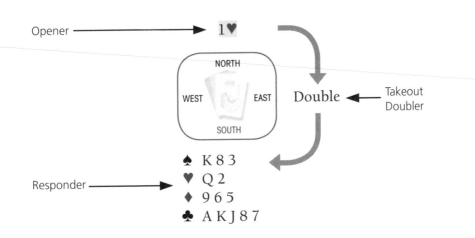

Opener → 1♥

NORTH

WEST EAST   Double ← Takeout Doubler

SOUTH

♠ K 8 3
Responder → ♥ Q 2
♦ 9 6 5
♣ A K J 8 7

Redouble. With 10 or more high-card points, responder starts with a redouble, or makes some form of artificial raise with a fit for opener's suit[5]. After a takeout double, a 2♣ response would be non-forcing and show a weaker hand.

Let's look at an example where responder is a passed hand:

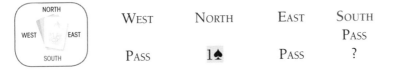

WEST	NORTH	EAST	SOUTH
			PASS
PASS	1♠	PASS	?

♠ 9 3
♥ 7 5
♦ A J 9 6 5
♣ K Q 8 4

Respond 2♦. Once South has passed initially, showing fewer than 13 points, a 2/1 response is no longer forcing to game. In fact, it's not even forcing! With a *light opening* bid in third or fourth position, opener can pass responder's new suit bid, hoping for a small partscore.

---

[5] Many partnerships use responder's jump to 2NT over a takeout double to show four-card or longer support for opener's suit and the values for a limit raise or better. This is known as Jordan, Truscott, or Dormer 2NT.

Summary

2/1 APPLIES WHEN:

- Opener bids 1♦, 1♥, or 1♠.
- The next player passes.
- Responder bids a new suit at the two level **without jumping**.
- Responder is an unpassed hand.

2/1 GAME FORCE

A non-jump, new suit by responder at the two level is forcing to at least game and shows:

- 13 or more points.
- 5+ cards for a 2♥ response.
- 4+ cards (rarely 3) for a 2♦ or 2♣ response.

ADVANTAGES OF 2/1 GAME FORCE

- Clarifies the bidding messages after a 2/1 response.
- Conserves bidding room to:
    - Allow the partnership to get to the best game.
    - Allow the partnership to explore slam possibilities.

WHEN 2/1 DOESN'T APPLY

- If responder's right-hand opponent overcalls or doubles.
- If responder is a passed hand.

Quiz – Part I

Playing 2/1 Game Force, what is the bidding message sent by South's bid (**signoff**, invitational, **forcing**, **marathon**)in each of the following auctions?

a)

WEST	NORTH	EAST	SOUTH
PASS	1♦	PASS	1♠?

_____

b)

WEST	NORTH	EAST	SOUTH
	1♠	PASS	2♥?

_____

c)

WEST	NORTH	EAST	SOUTH
	1NT	PASS	3NT?

_____

d)

WEST	NORTH	EAST	SOUTH
PASS	1♥	2♣	2♦?

_____

e)

WEST	NORTH	EAST	SOUTH
	1♠	DOUBLE	2♣?

_____

f)

WEST	NORTH	EAST	SOUTH
			PASS
PASS	1♠	PASS	2♥?

_____

g)

WEST	NORTH	EAST	SOUTH
	1♥	PASS	2♦
PASS	2NT	PASS	3♦?

_____

Answers to Quiz – Part I

a) **Forcing.** A new suit response at the one level shows about 6 or more points and is forcing for one round. Although North is forced to make a rebid, South doesn't have to make another bid unless opener makes a forcing rebid, such as a *jump shift* to 3♣ or a *reverse* to 2♥. If North makes a minimum rebid, such as 1NT, 2♦ or 2♠, South can pass with a minimum response. Similarly, since the partnership is not forced to game, North won't have to bid again unless South makes another forcing bid.

b) **Marathon.** If the partnership has agreed to play 2/1 Game Force, South's 2♥ response is forcing until at least the game level.

c) **Signoff.** North has already described the hand with the 1NT opening. That is all the information South needs to decide WHERE, notrump, and How HIGH, game. North is expected to pass. If South needed more information from North to decide on the contract, South would have made a forcing bid.

d) **Forcing.** After an opponent's overcall, responder's new-suit bid is still forcing, but it is not forcing to game, even if the partnership is playing 2/1 Game Force. 2/1 Game Force doesn't apply after an overcall.

e) **Invitational.** After a takeout double, responder's bid of a new suit at the two level is not forcing. With about 10 or more high-card points and a five-card or longer club suit, responder would start with a redouble. The 2♣ bid shows about 6–10 points and a good six-card or longer suit.

f) **Invitational.** Although a new suit by responder is usually forcing, that no longer applies once responder is a passed hand. South's initial pass shows fewer than 13 points, so South can't be in a position to commit the partnership to game after North's opening bid. Also, North might have opened *light* in third position, hoping for a small partscore contract.

g) **Marathon.** South's initial 2♦ response was a 2/1 game-forcing bid. So each subsequent bid by the partnership below the game level is a marathon bid. Neither partner can pass until at least a game contract is reached.

Quiz – Part II

North opens 1♥, and East passes. What does South respond with each of the following hands? What is the bidding message?

WEST	NORTH	EAST	SOUTH
	1♥	PASS	?

a) ♠ 7 5 2
♥ A 4
♦ K J 3
♣ K J 9 6 2

b) ♠ A 7
♥ 5
♦ A J 8 7 3
♣ A K Q 9 5

c) ♠ A Q J 9 4
♥ 7
♦ A Q 9 6 2
♣ J 4

d) ♠ A 8 3
♥ J 9 4
♦ 8 6 2
♣ A K J 4

e) ♠ J 9 7 3
♥ Q 4
♦ A K 9 6 5
♣ 7 4

f) ♠ A K 7 4
♥ 4
♦ J 8
♣ K Q 10 8 3 2

North opens 1♠, South responds 2♦, and North rebids 2♥. What rebid would South make with each of the following hands?

WEST	NORTH	EAST	SOUTH
	1♠	PASS	2♦
PASS	2♥	PASS	?

g) ♠ J 3
♥ A 4
♦ A Q J 10 7 3
♣ J 8 2

h) ♠ K 10 5
♥ 9 2
♦ K Q J 6 3
♣ A Q 2

i) ♠ 5
♥ Q 10 8 7
♦ A K 8 7 3
♣ A 6 2

j) ♠ 7 3
♥ A J 4
♦ Q J 9 7 2
♣ A Q 5

k) ♠ K 6 3
♥ K 10 7 5
♦ A K 9 5
♣ 7 3

l) ♠ J 4
♥ K Q 5
♦ A Q 8 7 3
♣ A Q 10

Answers to Quiz – Part II

a) **2♣**. With 12 high-card points plus 1 length point for the five-card club suit, South has enough to make a game-forcing response.

b) **2♦**. With two five-card suits, responder bids the higher-ranking first. The new suit response at the two level is game forcing.

c) **1♠**. South has 14 high-card points plus 1 length point for each of the five-card suits, more than enough to commit the partnership to game. However, South starts with a standard, forcing response of 1♠. A jump to 2♠ would be a jump shift, not a 2/1 Game Force.

d) **2♣**. A 2/1 response in a minor suit does not promise a five-card suit. South plans to show the heart support at the next opportunity.

e) **1♠**. With 10 high-card points plus 1 length point for the five-card diamond suit, South doesn't have enough strength to make a 2/1 game-forcing response of 2♦. Instead, South can bid the four-card spade suit at the one level. This is forcing for one round.

f) **2♣**. With enough for a 2/1 Game Force, South makes the descriptive response of 2♣, bidding the longer suit first. 2♣ is forcing to game.

g) **3♦**. Since the initial 2♦ response was forcing to game, South can simply rebid the six-card diamond suit. That's still game-forcing.

h) **2♠**. Having made a 2/1 game-forcing response, South can conveniently show the spade support at the two level, leaving plenty of room for the partnership to explore a possible slam.

i) **3♥**. South doesn't have to jump to game to show the heart support and game-going values. The initial 2♦ bid already committed the partnership to game.

j) **2NT**. Although South knows the partnership belongs in a game contract, there's no need to jump to 3NT after the original 2/1 Game Force. South can leave room to hear opener's next bid.

k) **3♥**. South was originally planning to show the spade support on the rebid, but opener's heart bid, showing at least five spades and four hearts, has given South another choice. In general, the 4-4 fit will play as well, or better, than the 5-3 fit. So South raises the second suit.

l) **2NT**. With 18 high-card points, South wants to make a slam try. There's still plenty of time, since the partnership is forced to at least game. South can wait to hear opener's next bid before making a move toward slam.

Quiz – Part III

How is the auction likely to go with the following hands if the partnership is playing 2/1 Game Force? How might the auction go using standard methods?

a)

OPENER	RESPONDER
♠ 4	♠ A 10 7
♥ K Q 7 6 5 2	♥ J 8
♦ A K 6 4	♦ Q 5 2
♣ 5 3	♣ K Q J 7 2

	OPENER	RESPONDER
2/1 Game Force:	_____	_____
	_____	_____
	_____	_____
Standard:	_____	_____
	_____	_____
	_____	_____

b)

OPENER	RESPONDER
♠ A Q	♠ 7 5 2
♥ A J 10 8 5 3 2	♥ K Q 4
♦ Q 3	♦ A K 10 7 2
♣ 7 6	♣ K Q

	OPENER	RESPONDER
2/1 Game Force:	_____	_____
	_____	_____
	_____	_____
	_____	_____
Standard:	_____	_____
	_____	_____

Answers to Quiz – Part III

a) Playing 2/1 the auction is likely to go:

OPENER	RESPONDER
1♥	2♣
2♦	2NT
3♥	4♥

After the 2/1 game-forcing 2♣ response, opener can comfortably show the diamonds. Responder can bid 2NT, describing the hand and giving opener an opportunity to further describe the hand. When opener shows the extra length in hearts, responder can place the contract in 4♥.

Using standard methods, the auction might go:

OPENER	RESPONDER
1♥	2♣
2♦	3NT
PASS?	

If opener chooses to show the second suit, responder can't afford to bid only 2NT since that would be invitational, not forcing. So responder jumps to 3NT. Now opener doesn't know whether to leave the partnership in 3NT or rebid the heart suit. Responder could have had a singleton, or even a void, in hearts.

b) Playing 2/1 the auction is likely to go:

OPENER	RESPONDER
1♥	2♦
2♥	3♥
3♠	4NT
5♥	6♥

When opener rebids the hearts, responder can raise to only 3♥, still forcing. This gives opener room to show the ♠A. Responder, satisfied that the opponents cannot take the first two spade tricks, can now use Blackwood to check for aces and bid the slam when opener shows two.

Using standard methods, the auction might go:

OPENER	RESPONDER
1♥	2♦
2♥	4♥

Since 2♦ isn't forcing to game, responder can't afford to bid only 3♥, but also doesn't want to jump right into Blackwood with no control in spades. Even if opener has two aces, the defenders may be able to take two or three spade tricks. Responder may settle for game in hearts, and the slam could be missed.

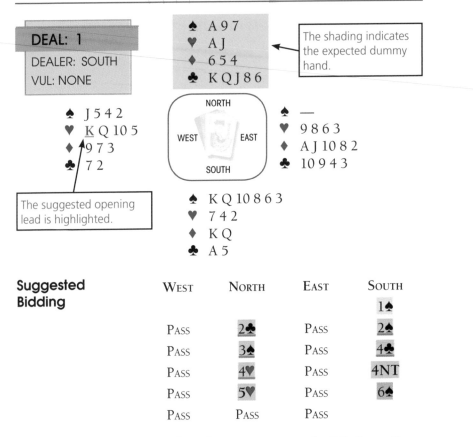

DEAL: 1

DEALER: SOUTH
VUL: NONE

♠ A 9 7
♥ A J
♦ 6 5 4
♣ K Q J 8 6

The shading indicates the expected dummy hand.

NORTH

WEST   EAST

SOUTH

♠ J 5 4 2
♥ K Q 10 5
♦ 9 7 3
♣ 7 2

♠ —
♥ 9 8 6 3
♦ A J 10 8 2
♣ 10 9 4 3

The suggested opening lead is highlighted.

♠ K Q 10 8 6 3
♥ 7 4 2
♦ K Q
♣ A 5

Suggested Bidding	WEST	NORTH	EAST	SOUTH
				1♠
	PASS	2♣	PASS	2♠
	PASS	3♠	PASS	4♣
	PASS	4♥	PASS	4NT
	PASS	5♥	PASS	6♠
	PASS	PASS	PASS	

After South opens 1♠, North's 2♣ response starts the 2/1 Game Force auction. South's 2♠ rebid is now forcing to game. It shows a six-card or longer suit, but says nothing about strength. North can simply raise to 3♠. This agrees on the trump suit and is forcing, giving the partnership room to determine whether it has the extra values to consider a slam.

On this deal, South has some extra values and now shows interest in slam by making a control-showing bid of 4♣. North cooperates by bidding 4♥. South can now visualize a slam if the partnership isn't missing two aces. Since the partnership can't make a control-showing bid to show the ace of the trump suit, South uses Blackwood, and bids 6♠ when the partnership is missing only one ace.

Suggested Opening Lead

West leads the ♥K, top of the broken sequence.

Suggested Play

The play looks straightforward, since declarer can count twelve winners: six spade tricks, the ♥A, and five club tricks. However, declarer must be careful not to lose two tricks: the ♦A, and a spade if the trumps break 4-0—and maybe a heart as well if the defenders gain the lead before declarer can discard the heart losers on the clubs. If declarer plays the ♠A at trick two, the contract can no longer be made. Instead, declarer should start with a low spade to the ♠K or ♠Q. Declarer can then pick up the whole spade suit if either defender shows out.

On the actual deal, when East shows out on the first round of spades, declarer finesses dummy's ♠9, cashes the ♠A, and crosses back to the ♣A to draw West's last trump. Declarer then takes the clubs, discarding the heart losers. Declarer loses only one diamond trick.

Suggested Defense

The lead of the ♥K sets up a potential winner for the defenders if they can regain the lead. That might occur if declarer mishandles the trump suit. The defenders will then get a spade, a heart, and a diamond trick.

Conclusion

In standard bidding, the auction might go:

West	North	East	South
			1♠
Pass	2♣	Pass	2♠
Pass	4♠?	Pass	Pass?
Pass			

North can't afford to bid only 3♠ since that would be invitational, not forcing. North has a little extra for the jump to 4♠, but can't really afford to go beyond game. North doesn't have enough to commit the partnership to slam, and Blackwood would not necessarily help. If South shows one ace, North won't know whether the defenders can take the first two, or three, diamond tricks. Similarly, South has some extra values, but not enough to move over North's jump to 4♠.

Using 2/1 saves space on the Bidding Ladder, allowing the partnership to exchange enough information to reach the excellent slam.

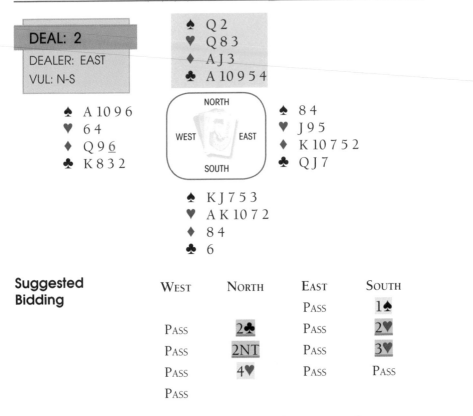

DEAL: 2

DEALER: EAST

VUL: N-S

♠ Q 2
♥ Q 8 3
♦ A J 3
♣ A 10 9 5 4

NORTH

♠ A 10 9 6
♥ 6 4
♦ Q 9 6
♣ K 8 3 2

WEST   EAST

♠ 8 4
♥ J 9 5
♦ K 10 7 5 2
♣ Q J 7

SOUTH

♠ K J 7 5 3
♥ A K 10 7 2
♦ 8 4
♣ 6

Suggested Bidding

WEST	NORTH	EAST	SOUTH
		PASS	1♠
PASS	2♣	PASS	2♥
PASS	2NT	PASS	3♥
PASS	4♥	PASS	PASS
PASS			

East passes. After South's 1♠ opening, North's 2♣ response is forcing to at least game. After opener rebids 2♥, North can afford to make a descriptive bid of 2NT. It is still forcing and gives South a chance to further describe the hand. When South rebids the hearts, showing a five-card suit, North puts the partnership in game in the eight-card heart fit.

Suggested Opening Lead

West has no clear cut opening lead. Probably leading the unbid suit is a reasonable choice. With a suit headed by an honor, West leads low, the ♦6.

Suggested Play

In 4♥, declarer has five heart tricks—assuming hearts are reasonably divided—, the ♦A, and the ♣A. Two extra tricks can be promoted in spades by driving out the ♠A. At least one more spade trick can be developed through length if the missing spades are divided 3-3 or 4-2.

After winning the ♦A, declarer should draw trumps—starting with the ♥K or ♥A and then over to the ♥Q, in case East holds four hearts including the ♥J. When the hearts divide 3-2, declarer can lead to dummy's ♠Q and back to the ♠J or ♠K to promote two winners in the suit by driving out the ♠A. After regaining the lead, declarer can take the remaining spade winner and give up a spade to West when the spade suit proves to be divided 4-2. That establishes declarer's fifth spade as a winner through length. On regaining the lead, declarer has ten tricks.

Suggested Defense

There's no defense to defeat 4♥. If North becomes declarer in 3NT, rather than South being declarer in 4♥, a diamond lead from East will defeat 3NT. If North wins the ♦A, West will eventually gain the lead with the ♠A and return a diamond. If North instead chooses to hold up twice with the ♦A, East can switch to the ♣Q after winning the second diamond trick to defeat the contract—two diamonds, two clubs, and the ♠A.

Conclusion

In standard bidding, the auction might go:

West	North	East	South
		Pass	1♠
Pass	2♣	Pass	2♥
Pass	3NT?	Pass	Pass?
Pass			

After South bids 2♥, North can't afford to bid 2NT since it would not be forcing. Knowing the partnership belongs in game and unaware that there is an eight-card major suit fit, North may simply choose to bid game in notrump. That leaves South in a quandary. 3NT could easily be the best spot if North doesn't have support for either hearts or spades. If South decides to pass, the partnership ends in a poor contract.

Using 2/1, opener had an easy time describing a hand with five spades and five hearts, helping responder choose the best game contract.

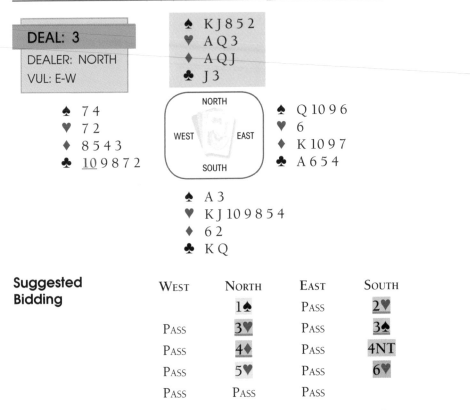

Suggested Bidding

WEST	NORTH	EAST	SOUTH
	1♠	PASS	2♥
PASS	3♥	PASS	3♠
PASS	4♦	PASS	4NT
PASS	5♥	PASS	6♥
PASS	PASS	PASS	

With 18 high-card points plus 1 length point for the five-card spade suit, North is too strong for 1NT and opens 1♠. After South responds 2♥, promising at least a five-card suit, the partnership is in a 2/1 auction. North raises to 3♥ to settle WHERE. The partnership is forced to game, so there is room left to consider How High—game or slam.

With extra values, South makes a move toward slam with the ♣A by making a control-showing bid of 3♠. The partnership has already found an eight-card or longer heart fit, so this is a control-showing bid, not trump agreement. There's no need to find two trump suits! South doesn't want to jump right to 4NT. North could have a minimum opening, and the partnership could have two diamond losers even if North shows two aces. Imagine North's ♦A being the ♣A.

North cooperates by showing the ♦A. With two low clubs, North can't launch into Blackwood because the partnership might have two club losers even if South shows one ace (imagine South having the ♦K instead of the ♣K). Once North shows something in diamonds, South can safely use Blackwood and reach the good slam contract.

Suggested Opening Lead

West would lead the ♣10, top of the sequence in the unbid suit.

Suggested Play

Declarer has ten top tricks: two spades, seven hearts, and the ♦A. An eleventh trick can be promoted in clubs by driving out the ♣A, so one more trick is needed. Declarer could try the 50% diamond finesse, but a better approach is to try to establish an extra spade winner through length.

Suppose the defenders start with two rounds of clubs. Declarer wins and draws two rounds of trumps, leaving a high trump in dummy as an entry. Then declarer plays the ♠A, ♠K, and ruffs a spade. When the spades don't break 3-3, declarer crosses to dummy with a trump and ruffs another spade. Now dummy's remaining spade is a winner. Declarer crosses to the ♦A, and discards a diamond on the spade winner. If the spades had broken 5-1, declarer could fall back on the diamond finesse.

Suggested Defense

There's no way to defeat the slam if declarer plays correctly. The best lead turns out to be a diamond. However, declarer should refuse the 50% diamond finesse, and hope to establish an extra trick in spades (over 80%).

Conclusion

In standard bidding, the auction might go:

West	North	East	South
	1♠	Pass	2♥
Pass	4♥?	Pass	Pass?
Pass			

North can't raise to only 3♥, since that would not be forcing. North has to jump to game to show the extra strength. That leaves South with a problem. South can't be sure exactly how much extra strength North has. Holding two low diamonds, South doesn't really have a good hand to use Blackwood, and may settle for game.

Using 2/1, both partners have room to show extra values, making it possible to reach the slam.

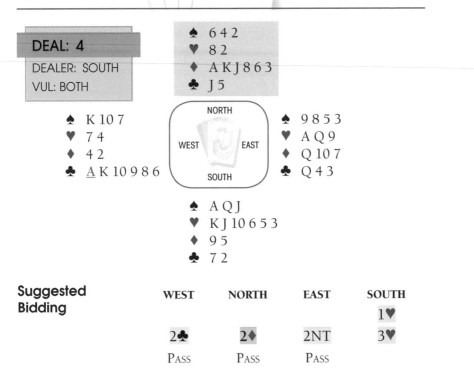

DEAL: 4

DEALER: SOUTH
VUL: BOTH

♠ 6 4 2
♥ 8 2
♦ A K J 8 6 3
♣ J 5

NORTH

♠ K 10 7
♥ 7 4
♦ 4 2
♣ A K 10 9 8 6

WEST   EAST

♠ 9 8 5 3
♥ A Q 9
♦ Q 10 7
♣ Q 4 3

SOUTH

♠ A Q J
♥ K J 10 6 5 3
♦ 9 5
♣ 7 2

Suggested Bidding

WEST	NORTH	EAST	SOUTH
			1♥
2♣	2♦	2NT	3♥
PASS	PASS	PASS	

After South opens the bidding 1♥ and West overcalls 2♣, North has to decide what to do. North has 9 high-card points plus 2 length points for the six-card diamond suit. That's enough to bid a new suit at the two level because 2/1 Game Force no longer applies after an overcall. North's 2♦ bid is forcing, but it is not forcing to game.

With 10 high-card points, a fit with partner's clubs, and stoppers in both the opponents' suits, hearts and diamonds, East has enough to suggest a game in notrump by bidding an invitational 2NT. South doesn't have to bid after East bids, but would likely choose to show the extra length in hearts by rebidding the heart suit.

South's 3♥ bid is not forcing, and might end the auction. Either West or East might choose to compete further, but their side is vulnerable and they may not want to get too high with both opponents bidding. North has nothing further to say, having already described the hand with the 2♦ bid.

Suggested Opening Lead

West will lead the ♣A, top of the touching cards.

Suggested Play

Declarer starts with a sure trick in spades and two in diamonds. The spade suit will provide at least one extra trick through promotion, and could provide two extra tricks with the help of a repeated finesse if East holds the ♠K. At least one trick can be promoted in hearts, and the suit should provide three more tricks through length if the missing hearts are divided 3-2.

Since there are two sure club losers and a heart loser, declarer can afford to lose a trick to the ♠K or the ♥Q, but not both. With only two entries to the dummy, the ♦A and ♦K, declarer will have to decide whether to try the heart finesse, hoping East has the ♥Q, or the spade finesse, hoping East has the ♠K. Since drawing trumps is a priority, and East is more likely to hold the ♥Q based on the 2NT bid, declarer will likely choose to use the entries to try the heart finesse. On the actual layout, the heart finesse works and that gives declarer nine tricks: two spades, five hearts, and two diamonds.

Suggested Defense

The defenders can't defeat 3♥ if declarer chooses to take the heart finesse, but can defeat the contract if declarer tries the spade finesse. The defenders will then get a spade, two hearts, and two clubs, since declarer won't have enough entries to take repeated heart finesses.

Conclusion

If North passes, East-West may buy the contract in 2NT, or perhaps even get to 3NT. If South leads a heart against a notrump contract, East can take nine tricks by winning the ♥Q and leading a spade toward dummy's ♠K. East-West will get a spade trick, two heart tricks, and six club tricks!

Responder does well to introduce the diamond suit after the 2♣ overcall. It helps the partnership compete for partscore or find the best defense if the opponents buy the contract.

All my life I've heard, "What if the best contract is one notrump?" That is true – sometimes one notrump is the best contract, or will go down the least. But what we forcing notrump players have going for us is that we can play all suit contracts, including the original major-suit opening; we can still arrive at games when responder has almost a two-over-one response; we can select our best suit fit; and much, much more.

—AL ROTH, PICTURE BIDDING (1991)

Roth, one of the game's greatest theorists and the player given credit for inventing the 1NT forcing response, is responding to those skeptics who ask: "What about playing in one notrump?"

The Forcing 1NT Response

If the partnership has agreed to play Two-Over-One Game Force (2/1), then a non-jump, new suit response at the two level is a marathon bid, showing 13 or more points. It's forcing to at least game. That can create a challenge for responder after the opening bid is 1♥ or 1♠ and responder has 11 or 12 points.

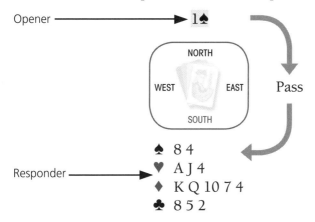

Opener ——————→ 1♠

NORTH

WEST   EAST   Pass

SOUTH

Responder ——————→
♠ 8 4
♥ A J 4
♦ K Q 10 7 4
♣ 8 5 2

Suppose responder, South, has this hand, worth 11 points—10 high-card points plus 1 length point for the five-card diamond suit. In standard methods, South is too strong to bid 1NT, which promises about 6–9 or 10 points, and would respond 2♦. Playing 2/1, however, a 2♦ response would promise an opening bid or better, and South isn't strong enough to commit the partnership to the game level.

To get around this dilemma, when playing 2/1, the range for a 1NT response has to be expanded from 6–10 to 6–12 points.

The Forcing 1NT Response

Allowing responder to have as many as 12 points for a response of 1NT creates another challenge for the partnership. In standard methods, opener would pass a 1NT response with a balanced hand of about 13–14 points since there is little danger of missing a game contract when responder has at most 10 points. If responder can have 11 or 12 points, however, there could be a combined total of 25 or 26 points, and the partnership could miss a game contract.

To meet this challenge, when playing 2/1, a response of 1NT to an opening bid of 1♥ or 1♠ is forcing—opener must bid again.

1NT FORCING

When the opening bid is 1♥ or 1♠ in first or second position, and the next player passes, a response of 1NT shows about 6–12 points and is forcing.

The 1NT response is forcing for only one round; it is not forcing to game.

The use of the forcing 1NT is not a big change from standard methods. Most of the time, the auction will go the same way in either system. Although a 1NT response is not forcing in standard methods, opener often bids again.

Let's consider some examples:

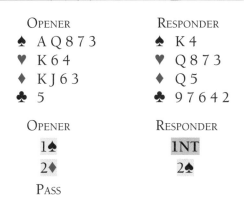

Opener	Responder
♠ A Q 8 7 3	♠ K 4
♥ K 6 4	♥ Q 8 7 3
♦ K J 6 3	♦ Q 5
♣ 5	♣ 9 7 6 4 2

Opener	Responder
1♠	1NT
2♦	2♠
Pass	

Opener starts with 1♠, the five-card major suit. With only 7 high-card points, responder isn't strong enough to do anything but respond 1NT. Opener now shows the second suit. Responder gives *preference* back to opener's first suit, spades, and the partnership stops in partscore.

Even though the partnership is in a seven-card spade fit, it's a good spot, probably better than 1NT or 2♥ on the 4-3 fit. Playing 2/1 or standard—or almost any other methods—the partnership would reach the same contract.

Opener	Responder
♠ K J 3	♠ A 5 2
♥ A K J 10 7 5	♥ 6 2
♦ 3	♦ 10 7 4
♣ A 9 3	♣ K J 6 5 2

Opener	Responder
1♥	1NT
3♥	4♥
Pass	

After the forcing 1NT response, opener shows a medium-strength hand of about 17–18 points and a good six-card or longer heart suit with a jump rebid in hearts. With 8 high-card points plus 1 length point for the five-card club suit, responder has enough to accept the invitation and bid game.

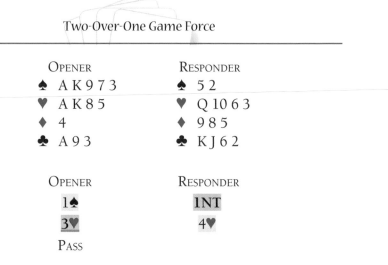

	Opener	Responder
♠	A K 9 7 3	5 2
♥	A K 8 5	Q 10 6 3
♦	4	9 8 5
♣	A 9 3	K J 6 2

Opener	Responder
1♠	1NT
3♥	4♥
Pass	

Over the forcing 1NT response, opener makes a strong jump shift to 3♥, showing a maximum-strength opening bid. Since the jump shift is a marathon bid, responder bids again, and the partnership reaches a reasonable game contract.

On some hands, the forcing 1NT response will make a difference to the auction, and opener has to know how to deal with a hand that would be passed playing standard methods[6].

---

[6] A review of opener's standard rebids after a 1NT response can be found in Appendix 2.

Opener's Rebid with a Minimum Balanced Hand

Whenever we change our bidding methods, some auctions will seem a little strange at first. When responder bids 1NT, opener probably won't want to bid again with a minimum balanced hand where it seems that 1NT might be the best contract[7].

West (Opener)	North	East (Responder)	South
1♠	Pass	1NT	Pass
?			

♠ A Q 8 7 3
♥ K 6 4
♦ K J 6
♣ 5 3

Using standard methods, with a minimum balanced hand and no second suit to show, opener would pass a non-forcing 1NT response with this hand. Playing 2/1, opener can't pass because the 1NT response is forcing. What does opener rebid?

OPENER'S MINOR REBID

After a forcing 1NT, with a minimum balanced hand opener bids:
- The longer minor suit, or
- 2♣ with equal length.

Instead of rebidding 2♠, which would tend to show a six-card or longer suit, opener would rebid 2♦ on this hand. This is similar to an opening bid of 1♣ or 1♦, which could be based on a three-card suit.

West (Opener)	North	East (Responder)	South
1♥	Pass	1NT	Pass
?			

♠ 9 8
♥ A K 8 7 5
♦ A J 4
♣ J 9 3

Rebid 2♣. With a choice of three-card minors, standard practice is to rebid 2♣. Responder will be aware that you might have been forced to bid a weak three-card suit.

---

[7] A variation of the Forcing 1NT response, 1NT semi-forcing, is discussed in Appendix 3

Advantages of 1NT Forcing

Although it may seem to be a disadvantage for opener to have to bid again after a forcing 1NT response when 1NT could be the best spot, the partnership will often find a better contract than using standard methods. For example, these might be the combined hands:

OPENER	RESPONDER
♠ A Q 8 7 3	♠ K 2
♥ K 6 4	♥ Q 8 3
♦ K J 6	♦ Q 10 7 5 3
♣ 5 3	♣ 9 6 4

Using standard methods, the auction would go:

OPENER	RESPONDER
1♠	1NT
PASS	

With a balanced minimum, opener would pass the invitational, but non-forcing, 1NT response.

Playing 2/1 with a forcing 1NT response, the auction would go:

OPENER	RESPONDER
♠ A Q 8 7 3	♠ K 2
♥ K 6 4	♥ Q 8 3
♦ K J 6	♦ Q 10 7 5 3
♣ 5 3	♣ 9 6 4

OPENER	RESPONDER
1♠	1NT
2♦	PASS

2♦ is actually a better contract than 1NT.

Let's change responder's hand:

Opener	Responder
♠ A Q 8 7 3	♠ 6 2
♥ K 6 4	♥ Q J 9 8 7 3
♦ K J 6	♦ Q 3
♣ 5 3	♣ 9 6 4

Using standard methods, the auction would go:

Opener	Responder
1♠	1NT
Pass	

Using a forcing 1NT response, the auction would go:

Opener	Responder
♠ A Q 8 7 3	♠ 6 2
♥ K 6 4	♥ Q J 9 8 7 3
♦ K J 6	♦ Q 3
♣ 5 3	♣ 9 6 4

Opener	Responder
1♠	1NT
2♦	2♥
Pass	

Responder doesn't have enough strength to bid 2♥ directly over opener's 1♠ bid. Once opener bids 2♦, however, responder has an opportunity to show the heart suit. Even though it is a new suit by responder, it is not forcing.

Opener now knows responder has a good five-card or a six-card or longer heart suit, but a hand too weak to make a 2/1 response. So opener is comfortable passing, leaving the partnership in a partscore in responder's long suit. 2♥ is a much better spot than 1NT.

Responder's Rebid with 6–10 Points

After making a forcing 1NT response to opener's 1♥ or 1♠ bid, responder's rebid with about 6–10 points essentially follows along the lines of standard methods. For example, if opener shows no additional strength by simply rebidding the major suit at the two level, or bidding a lower-ranking new suit at the two level[8], responder can:

- Pass, if opener has rebid the major or shown a lower-ranking second suit which responder prefers.
- Give preference back to opener's original suit if opener has shown a second suit.
- Raise opener's second suit with a good fit and about 8–10 points, the top of the 6–10 point range, where game is still a possibility.
- Bid a new suit with a good five-card or longer suit and little or no support for opener's suits.

The only impact of the forcing 1NT is that responder should be cautious about passing opener's minor-suit rebid, since it might be a three-card suit.

Let's look at examples of each of responder's options.

---

[8] A reverse by opener is forcing for one round. This only occurs after a major suit opening if the opening bid is 1♥ and opener then bids 2♠ over the forcing 1NT response.

PASSING

When opener rebids the major suit, showing a six-card or longer suit but a minimum opening bid of about 13–16 points, responder usually passes[9].

OPENER	RESPONDER
♠ K J 10 9 7 6 3	♠ 2
♥ K 6	♥ Q J 7 3
♦ 3	♦ A 9 6 5
♣ A 6 4	♣ Q 8 5 2

OPENER	RESPONDER
1♠	1NT
2♠	PASS

With a misfit for opener's suit, responder should not consider bidding again. 2NT would show a stronger hand—which will be discussed shortly. Also, 2NT would be an inferior contract to 2♠.

When opener bids a second suit, responder can pass with a definite preference for the second suit, especially when responder has a total misfit for opener's first suit.

OPENER	RESPONDER
♠ A J 7 6 3	♠ 5
♥ K Q 6 2	♥ J 9 7
♦ 5 2	♦ Q 9 6 3
♣ A 4	♣ K 8 7 5 3

OPENER	RESPONDER
1♠	1NT
2♥	PASS

Opener's 2♥ rebid could show a four-card suit. However, with a singleton spade, responder has no better choice than passing and hoping for the best. Again, responder should not consider bidding 2NT. It risks getting the partnership much too high.

---

[9] The only exceptions are when responder might choose to raise with a doubleton high honor in opener's suit and a maximum, or when responder has a singleton or void in opener's major and a very long suit that responder prefers as trumps.

GIVING PREFERENCE

When opener shows a second suit—especially a minor, which could be a three-card suit—responder should always give preference back to the first suit with equal length, and usually give preference back to the first suit with one or even two more cards in the second suit! Going back to opener's first suit when holding more cards in the second suit is called *false preference*.

OPENER	RESPONDER
♠ A 8 4	♠ K 9 7
♥ K Q 10 7 5	♥ J 4
♦ 7 3	♦ J 9 6 5 2
♣ Q J 6	♣ K 7 3

OPENER	RESPONDER
1♥	1NT
2♣	2♥
PASS	

By returning to hearts, opener's known five-card major suit, responder avoids leaving the partnership in clubs, a six-card trump fit.

Giving false preference is also a good idea because opener's rebid of a new lower-ranking suit shows anywhere from about 13–18 points, just short of the strength needed for a game-forcing strong jump shift. By giving preference back to opener's first suit, responder provides opener an opportunity to show extra strength or distribution.

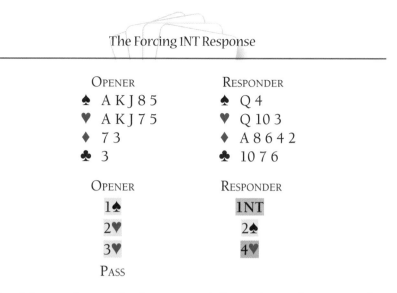

OPENER	RESPONDER
♠ A K J 8 5	♠ Q 4
♥ A K J 7 5	♥ Q 10 3
♦ 7 3	♦ A 8 6 4 2
♣ 3	♣ 10 7 6

OPENER	RESPONDER
1♠	1NT
2♥	2♠
3♥	4♥
PASS	

By giving preference back to opener's first suit, spades, responder gives opener an opportunity to further describe the hand by rebidding hearts to show a five-card suit. Opener also shows some extra strength by bidding 3♥; with a minimum hand, opener would pass. With useful cards in both hearts and spades, along with the ♦A, responder takes the partnership to the excellent game.

RAISING OPENER'S SECOND SUIT

With 6–10 points, responder usually settles for partscore when opener doesn't promise more than a minimum. Still, opener's bid of a new suit at the two level covers a wide range of 13–18 points, so game may still be possible when responder is at the top of the range.

OPENER	RESPONDER
♠ K Q 10 7 5	♠ J 4
♥ A J 8 5	♥ K Q 7 3
♦ A 7	♦ 6 4 3
♣ Q 4	♣ K J 7 2

OPENER	RESPONDER
1♠	1NT
2♥	3♥
4♥	PASS

With 10 high-card points, responder bids 1NT over opener's 1♠. When opener shows hearts, however, responder has a good fit and enough to invite game. With more than a minimum, opener accepts the invitation, and the partnership reaches a good game contract.

OPENER	RESPONDER
♠ A K 10 5 3	♠ 6 2
♥ A J 5	♥ 10 4 2
♦ J 7 4 3	♦ K Q 10 8 6
♣ K	♣ A 10 3

OPENER	RESPONDER
1♠	1NT
2♦	3♦
3NT	PASS

With 9 high-card points and 1 length point for the five-card diamond suit, responder chooses to raise to 3♦ with the excellent support. With extra strength, opener decides to go for the nine-trick game of 3NT rather than 5♦—although 5♦ is also an excellent contract on the combined hands. With a weaker hand, without the ♥A, perhaps, opener would pass and the partnership will stop in a partscore of 3♦.

BIDDING A NEW SUIT

Since responder's 1NT response has denied enough strength to make a 2/1 game forcing bid in a new suit, responder can now bid a new suit without committing the partnership to game. Responder should use this prudently, since opener is unlikely to have a fit with responder's suit when opener has rebid the original major suit or bid a second suit. Still, it is sometimes responder's best option.

OPENER	RESPONDER
♠ A 8 3	♠ K 9 5
♥ K J 9 7 5	♥ 4
♦ 8	♦ Q 10 9 7 6 5 3
♣ A J 6 4	♣ Q 2

OPENER	RESPONDER
1♥	1NT
2♣	2♦
PASS	

Responder doesn't have enough to make a 2/1 response of 2♦ over the opening bid of 1♥. So responder starts with a forcing 1NT. Opener bids the second suit. With no fit with either of opener's suits, responder suggests diamonds as the trump suit. Opener doesn't particularly like diamonds, but has no extra values and has already shown a five-card heart suit and three or more clubs. Knowing responder likely has a weak hand with a good five-card suit or six or more diamonds, opener passes and hopes for the best. The partnership lands in its best contract.

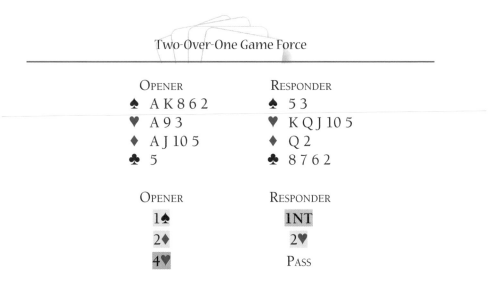

OPENER	RESPONDER
♠ A K 8 6 2	♠ 5 3
♥ A 9 3	♥ K Q J 10 5
♦ A J 10 5	♦ Q 2
♣ 5	♣ 8 7 6 2

OPENER	RESPONDER
1♠	1NT
2♦	2♥
4♥	PASS

Over 1♠, responder doesn't have enough to bid 2♥, and settles for a forcing 1NT response. Opener doesn't have quite enough to jump shift to 3♦, and so simply shows the second suit by bidding 2♦. Responder could give simple preference back to 2♠, but with such a strong five-card heart suit, decides to suggest hearts as the trump suit. With a great fit for hearts, 16 high-card points, and a singleton club, opener puts the partnership in game.

SHOWING A WEAK RAISE OF OPENER'S MAJOR SUIT

Experienced partnerships might want to use the forcing 1NT to differentiate between a sound and a weak raise of opener's major.

With about 8–10 points, responder raises to the two level right away.

OPENER	RESPONDER
♠ A 4	♠ Q 6 5
♥ K Q 8 7 3	♥ A 6 4
♦ 7 3	♦ 9 8 5 2
♣ A Q J 5	♣ K 9 4

OPENER	RESPONDER
1♥	2♥
3♥	4♥
PASS	

Responder's immediate raise to 2♥ shows some interest in game. With 16 high-card points plus 1 length point, opener will make a move toward game[10]. With the top of the range, responder will likely accept the invitation, and the partnership reaches a sound game contract.

With a weak raise, about 5–7 points, responder bids 1NT and then gives preference to the major suit.

OPENER	RESPONDER
♠ A 4	♠ Q 6 5
♥ K Q 8 7 3	♥ 9 6 4
♦ 7 3	♦ J 8 5 2
♣ A Q J 5	♣ K 9 4

OPENER	RESPONDER
1♥	1NT
2♣	2♥
PASS?	

With only 6 points, responder starts with 1NT, despite the three-card support. After opener bids 2♣, responder gives a weak-sounding preference to 2♥. This is likely to discourage opener from moving toward game.

---

[10] Depending on partnership methods, opener might make a game try of 3♣, for example.

Responder's Rebid with 11–12 Points

With 11 or 12 points, responder must make a move toward game after the forcing 1NT response, even if opener has not promised anything more than a minimum opening bid. There is likely to be a game, unless opener has a bare minimum or the hands don't fit well together. With about 11–12 points responder can:

- Rebid 2NT to show about 11–12 high-card points.
- Make a three-card limit raise of opener's major.
- Jump in a new suit to show a good six-card or longer suit.
- Raise opener's second suit.

Let's look at examples of each option.

REBIDDING 2NT

With a balanced, or semi-balanced hand, 11–12 high-card points, and stoppers in the unbid suits, responder can move toward game over opener's rebid at the two level by bidding 2NT.

OPENER	RESPONDER
♠ J 3	♠ A Q 9
♥ K Q 10 6 3	♥ J 4
♦ A K Q 5	♦ J 9 2
♣ 8 6	♣ Q J 10 7 3

OPENER	RESPONDER
1♥	1NT
2♦	2NT
3NT	PASS

With 11 high-card points plus 1 length point for the five-card club suit, responder starts with a forcing 1NT response. After hearing opener's rebid, responder invites game by bidding 2NT. With extra values, opener accepts the invitation, and the partnership reaches its best spot, 3NT.

Note that responder's 2NT bid after the forcing 1NT bid is a strong invitation to game, showing 11–12 points, not 6–10 pts.

MAKING A THREE-CARD LIMIT RAISE

The forcing 1NT response provides an easy way for responder to show three-card support for opener's major with an invitational hand, about 11–12 points.

OPENER	RESPONDER
♠ K Q 8 7 3	♠ A J 2
♥ 4 2	♥ Q 8 7 3
♦ Q 5	♦ K J 6 2
♣ A J 7 4	♣ 8 3

In standard methods after a 1♠ opening, responder would start with a 2♦ response, since an immediate limit raise to 3♠ would show four-card support. This would create a rebid challenge for opener, since a bid of 3♣ would tend to show extra strength and commit the partnership to game. The partnership is likely to get too high.

In 2/1, the auction would go:

OPENER	RESPONDER
1♠	1NT
2♣	3♠
PASS	

Responder starts with a forcing 1NT. After opener's 2♣ rebid, responder jumps to 3♠ to show an invitational hand of about 11–12 points with specifically three-card spade support. With four-card support, responder would immediately jump to 3♠ as a limit raise. Opener passes with a minimum and the partnership stops in a reasonable spot.

Let's give opener a slightly better hand:

OPENER	RESPONDER
♠ K Q 8 7 3	♠ A J 2
♥ 4 2	♥ Q 8 7 3
♦ Q 5	♦ K J 6 2
♣ A K 7 4	♣ 8 3

OPENER	RESPONDER
1♠	1NT
2♣	3♠
4♠	PASS

Now opener has enough to accept the invitation, and the excellent game contract is reached.

If opener has bid the major suit only once, responder jumps to the three level to show a three-card limit raise. If opener rebids the major suit at the two level, responder simply raises to the three level to invite game.

OPENER	RESPONDER
♠ Q 4	♠ K 9 3
♥ K Q 10 7 3 2	♥ J 9 6
♦ J 5	♦ A 9 7 6
♣ K 8 4	♣ Q J 5

OPENER	RESPONDER
1♥	1NT
2♥	3♥
PASS	

Responder planned to jump to 3♥ if opener rebid 2♣ or 2♦. When opener rebids 2♥, responder sends a similar message by raising to 3♥. Holding a minimum, opener rejects the invitation, and the partnership stops in partscore.

When opener rebids the major, responder's raise to the three level doesn't guarantee three-card support. Consider these combined hands:

OPENER	RESPONDER
♠ Q 4	♠ K 9 3
♥ K Q 10 7 3 2	♥ J 9
♦ K 5	♥ A 9 7 6
♣ K 8 4	♣ Q J 6 5

OPENER	RESPONDER
1♥	1NT
2♥	3♥
4♥	PASS

Once opener rebids the hearts, responder can make an invitational raise to 3♥ with only a doubleton heart and 11 high-card points. Opener can't be sure whether responder has two or three hearts in this sequence, but knows there is at least an eight-card fit. With more than a bare minimum, opener would accept the invitation, and the partnership reaches a good game contract.

JUMPING IN A NEW SUIT[11]

With a good six-card or longer suit, responder can jump to the three level[12] in the suit as a strong invitation to game.

OPENER	RESPONDER
♠ K Q 9 7 5	♠ 6
♥ 8	♥ K J 10 9 7 6
♦ A K 9 5	♦ 7 4 3
♣ J 8 3	♣ A Q 7

OPENER	RESPONDER
1♠	1NT
2♦	3♥
PASS	

With 10 high-card points plus 2 length points for the six-card heart suit, responder doesn't quite have enough to respond 2♥. After the 2♦ rebid, responder makes a strong invitation by jumping to 3♥. With a minimum and a poor fit, opener passes. Opener doesn't bid 3NT with a singleton heart to 'improve' the contract. 3♥ is an excellent spot.

OPENER	RESPONDER
♠ K 3	♠ Q 10 8
♥ A Q 8 7 5	♥ 9 2
♦ Q 3	♦ A K J 8 7 5
♣ K J 6 2	♣ 5 4

OPENER	RESPONDER
1♥	1NT
2♣	3♦
3NT	PASS

Responder isn't strong enough for a 2/1 2♦ response, but can show the near game-forcing hand with a jump to 3♦ after originally bidding a forcing 1NT. With some extra strength, opener takes the partnership to the most likely game contract, 3NT.

---

[11] An alternative approach is discussed in Appendix 4.

[12] Hands where responder has no room to jump to the three level are discussed in Appendix 4.

RAISING OPENER'S SECOND SUIT

When opener bids a second suit over the forcing 1NT response, responder can raise with about 11–12 points to invite game.

Opener	Responder
♠ K Q 10 7 4	♠ J 3
♥ K Q 7 3	♥ A 8 6 2
♦ 8 3	♦ A 10 7 5
♣ A 4	♣ Q 9 6

Opener	Responder
1♠	1NT
2♥	3♥
4♥	Pass

When opener shows the hearts, responder raises to invite game. Knowing responder has about 11–12 points, opener accepts.

Reponder must be cautious when opener's second suit is a minor, since it could be a three-card suit. Responder should generally have five-card support to raise.

Opener	Responder
♠ A 9 5	♠ K Q 2
♥ A J 8 6 3	♥ 9 5
♦ 8 4	♦ 10 6 2
♣ K 8 4	♣ A J 9 7 5

Opener	Responder
1♥	1NT
2♣	3♣
Pass	

Responder's 1NT is forcing. With only five hearts, opener bids the three-card club suit. With 10 high-card points plus 1 length point for the fifth spade, responder has too much to pass. Opener could have as many as 18 points for the 2♣ rebid. Responder raises to invite game. With a minimum, opener passes. Opener isn't concerned about holding only three clubs. Responder is aware of this possibility.

With a very good fit for opener's second suit, responder can revalue the hand and make a jump raise.

Opener	Responder
♠ K J 7 5 2	♠ Q 3
♥ Q 8 6 2	♥ K J 10 7 5
♦ A Q	♦ K J 8 5 2
♣ 9 3	♣ 8

Opener	Responder
1♠	1NT
2♥	4♥
Pass	

Responder doesn't have enough strength to make a 2/1 response over the 1♠ opening, but when opener shows a heart suit, responder's hand becomes too strong for an invitational raise to 3♥. Responder raises all the way to game. If responder had raised to only 3♥, opener would likely have rejected the invitation, and the excellent game would be missed.

Opener	Responder
♠ A J 7 6 3	♠ Q 2
♥ 9 5	♥ 4
♦ A Q 10 6	♦ K 9 7 5 4 2
♣ K 2	♣ A 10 7 3

Opener	Responder
1♠	1NT
2♦	4♦
5♦	Pass

With a super hand for diamonds, responder makes a highly-invitational jump raise to 4♦. With a little extra, opener accepts, and the partnership reaches the excellent game contract. If responder had raised to only 3♦, opener would likely have settled for partscore.

When 1NT Forcing Doesn't Apply

Even if the partnership has agreed to play the Forcing 1NT response, there are three situations when it doesn't apply:

WHEN 1NT FORCING DOESN'T APPLY

- After an opening bid of 1♣ or 1♦.
- If responder's right-hand opponent overcalls or doubles.
- If responder is a passed hand.

AFTER AN OPENING BID OF 1♣ OR 1♦

When the opening bid is 1♥ or 1♠, responder's only option with 11–12 points is usually 1NT, since a new suit at the two level requires 13 or more points. So a response of 1NT is treated as forcing over 1♥ or 1♠, to give responder a chance to further describe the hand.

When the opening bid is 1♣, responder can bid diamonds, hearts, or spades at the one level. With no major, responder can show a balanced hand of about 11–12 points by jumping to 2NT[13], invitational. With a balanced hand of 13–15 points, responder can jump to 3NT. So there's little need to use a response of 1NT as forcing.

After an opening bid of 1♦, responder can bid hearts or spades at the one level. With a balanced hand and no major suit, responder can jump to 2NT with 11-12 points and 3NT with 13-15 points. The only suit responder can't show at the one level is clubs. Again, there is little need for a response of 1NT to be forcing.

So after an opening bid of 1♣ or 1♦, a response of 1NT shows about 6–10 points and is non-forcing.

---

[13] Over a 1♥ or 1♠ opening, many partnerships use a 2NT response to show a forcing major-suit raise (Jacoby 2NT). So this bid can't be used to show a balanced 11–12 points after 1♥ or 1♠. Instead, responder starts with a forcing 1NT response.

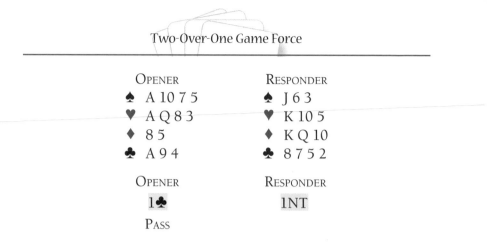

OPENER	RESPONDER
♠ A 10 7 5	♠ J 6 3
♥ A Q 8 3	♥ K 10 5
♦ 8 5	♦ K Q 10
♣ A 9 4	♣ 8 7 5 2

OPENER	RESPONDER
1♣	1NT
PASS	

Responder doesn't need to raise clubs with poor four-card support. Instead, responder bids 1NT, showing 6–10 points. Opener knows the partnership doesn't have a major-suit fit, since responder didn't bid 1♥ or 1♠. Opener is happy to play in a partscore in 1NT.

OPENER	RESPONDER
♠ A 5	♠ K 7 6
♥ A 8 3 2	♥ K 9 4
♦ K Q 10 4	♦ J 3
♣ 8 4 2	♣ A 10 7 5 3

OPENER	RESPONDER
1♦	2NT
PASS	

After the opening bid of 1♦, there is no need for a forcing 1NT response when responder has a balanced hand of 11–12 points[14]. Responder can jump to 2NT to show a balanced hand with invitational values[15] and no four-card or longer major suit. With a minimum, opener passes, and the partnership is in the best spot.

---

[14] Appendix 4 discusses methods for handling an unbalanced hand of 11-12 points with clubs when the opening bid is 1♦. A method for handling raises of opener's minor suit with 11 or more points is discussed in Appendix 5, Inverted Minor Suit Raises.

[15] Some partnerships prefer to treat the 2NT response as forcing, showing 13–15 points, and a jump to 3NT as 16–17 points. However, this makes it awkward to show a balanced hand with 11–12 points without adding additional agreements. The recommended approach is straightforward and popular.

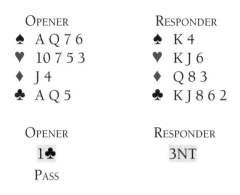

OPENER	RESPONDER
♠ A Q 7 6	♠ K 4
♥ 10 7 5 3	♥ K J 6
♦ J 4	♦ Q 8 3
♣ A Q 5	♣ K J 8 6 2

OPENER	RESPONDER
1♣	3NT
PASS	

After the opening bid of 1♣, responder can jump to 3NT with a balanced hand of 13–15 points, no four-card or longer major suit, and some strength in each of the unbid suits.

WHEN RESPONDER'S RIGHT-HAND OPPONENT OVERCALLS

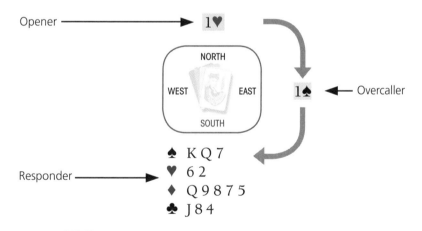

Respond 1NT. After East's overcall, South's 1NT response is natural and non-forcing. It shows about 6–10 points with at least one stopper in spades, the opponent's suit.

If the overcall is at the two level or higher, responder's notrump bids are also natural. A response of 2NT shows about 11–12 points; a response of 3NT shows about 13–15 points.

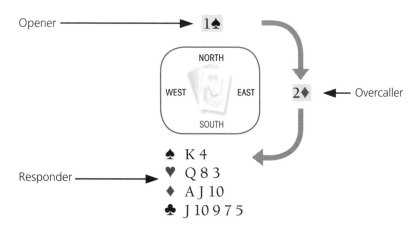

Opener — 1♠

NORTH

WEST   EAST   2♦ ← Overcaller

SOUTH

Responder —
♠ K 4
♥ Q 8 3
♦ A J 10
♣ J 10 9 7 5

Respond 2NT. This shows some strength in diamonds, the overcalled suit, and enough strength to invite opener to game.

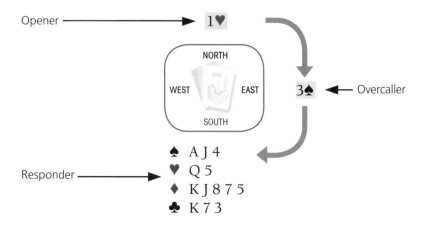

Opener — 1♥

NORTH

WEST   EAST   3♠ ← Overcaller

SOUTH

Responder —
♠ A J 4
♥ Q 5
♦ K J 8 7 5
♣ K 7 3

Respond 3NT. East's preemptive jump overcall has taken away the room to make a 2/1 game-forcing response of 2♦. Instead, settle for a descriptive 3NT bid.

WHEN RESPONDER'S RIGHT-HAND OPPONENT DOUBLES

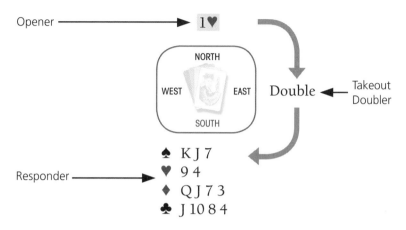

Respond 1NT. After East's takeout double, South's 1NT response is natural and non-forcing. 1NT shows a balanced hand with about 6–10 points.

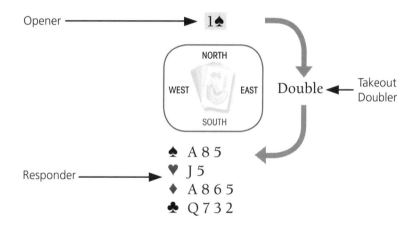

Redouble. After the double, responder starts with a redouble, showing 10 or more high-card points. South still plans to show the spade support at the next opportunity

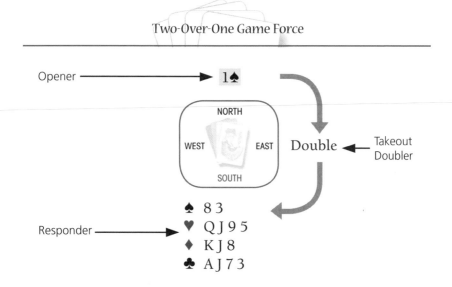

Redouble. Over the double, responder redoubles. There is a good chance North-South might be able to double any bid by the opponents for penalty.

WHEN RESPONDER IS A PASSED HAND

WEST	NORTH	EAST	SOUTH	
			PASS	
PASS	1♠	PASS	?	

♠ 6
♥ Q 10 7 3
♦ K 8 6 5 2
♣ J 6 4

Respond 1NT. This is the same response South would make if North opened 1♠ in first or second position. The difference is that, since South passed originally, the 1NT response is not forcing. As in standard, it simply shows about 6–10 points. Opener can pass with a minimum balanced hand.

Since the 1NT response to a major suit is no longer forcing when responder is a passed hand, the partnership has to consider how to handle this type of hand.

WEST	NORTH	EAST	SOUTH
			PASS
PASS	1♥	PASS	?

♠ 8 5 2
♥ A J 3
♦ K J 9 2
♣ Q 7 5

3♥? With 11 points but only three-card support for opener's major, this hand isn't really suitable for an immediate limit raise. There is also some danger that North has opened light in third position and a jump raise to 3♥ might get the partnership overboard. Opposite a first or second position opening, responder could start with a forcing 1NT and show the support later. Here, however, a 1NT response would not be forcing. Also a new-suit response would not be forcing. So responder is faced with a difficult choice.

To get around this dilemma, some partnerships continue to treat the 1NT response to a major as forcing, even when responder is a passed hand. A more popular approach, however, is to use the *Drury* convention over a 1♥ or 1♠ opening in third or fourth position[16]. A response of 2♣ is artificial and shows at least three-card support for opener's major and about 10 or more points, counting distribution. The partnership can then stop at the two level in the major suit when opener has no interest in getting to game.

---

[16] The Drury convention is described in Appendix 6.

Summary

1NT FORCING

When the opening bid is 1♥ or 1♠ in first or second position, and the next player passes, a response of 1NT shows about 6–12 points and is forcing.

OPENER'S REBID AFTER A FORCING 1NT

Opener makes the same rebid as after a non-forcing 1NT response except when holding a minimum balanced hand of 12–14 points. Instead of passing, opener bids:
- The longer minor suit, or
- 2♣ with equal length.

RESPONDER'S REBID AFTER A FORCING 1NT RESPONSE

After opener makes a minimum-strength rebid:

With 6–10 points:
- Pass.
- Give preference to opener's first suit.
- Bid a new suit.
- Raise to the three level with the top of the range.

With 11–12 points:
- Bid 2NT.
- Jump in a new suit to the three level (if possible).
- Make a three-card limit raise of opener's major.
- Raise opener's second suit.

WHEN 1NT FORCING DOESN'T APPLY

- After an opening bid of 1♣ or 1♦.
- If responder's right-hand opponent overcalls or doubles.
- If responder is a passed hand.

Quiz – Part I

Playing 2/1 Game Force, what is the bidding message sent by North's bid in each of the following auctions (**signoff**, invitational, **forcing**, **marathon**)?

a)
WEST	NORTH	EAST	SOUTH
		PASS	1♠
PASS	1NT?		

---

b)
WEST	NORTH	EAST	SOUTH
	PASS	PASS	1♥
PASS	1NT?		

---

c)
WEST	NORTH	EAST	SOUTH
			1♦
PASS	1NT?		

---

d)
WEST	NORTH	EAST	SOUTH
			1♣
PASS	2NT?		

---

e)
WEST	NORTH	EAST	SOUTH
		PASS	1♥
1♠	1NT?		

---

f)
WEST	NORTH	EAST	SOUTH
			1♠
DOUBLE	INT?		

---

g)
WEST	NORTH	EAST	SOUTH
		PASS	1♠
PASS	1NT	PASS	2♦
PASS	2♥?		

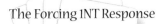

Answers to Quiz – Part I

a) **Forcing**. Playing 2/1 Game Force, a 1NT response to a major suit is forcing for one round in a non-competitive auction, when responder is an unpassed hand.

b) Invitational. After North passes originally, the 1NT response to a major suit opening is no longer forcing. South can pass with a minimum balanced hand. South might have opened 'light' in third position, hoping for a small partscore.

c) Invitational. A 1NT response to a minor suit opening is not forcing when playing 2/1 Game Force. It is the same response as in standard methods, showing about 6–10 points and no four-card or longer major suit.

d) Invitational. The recommended treatment is that a jump to 2NT in response to a minor suit opening shows an invitational hand with about 11–12 points. Again, responder denies a four-card or longer major suit.

e) Invitational. After an opponent's overcall, responder's 1NT response is no longer forcing. It shows about 6–10 points with at least one stopper in the opponent's suit.

f) Invitational. After a takeout double, responder's 1NT bid is also natural and non-forcing, showing about 6–10 points.

g) Invitational. Responder is showing a hand that was too weak to make an immediate response of 2♥, which would have been game-forcing. So responder likely has a six-card or longer heart suit, or possibly a good five-card heart suit, with about 6–10 points. With 11–12 points, responder could have jumped to 3♥.

Quiz – Part II

North opens 1♥, and East passes. What does South respond with each of the following hands?

WEST	NORTH	EAST	SOUTH
	1♥	PASS	?

a) ♠ A J 5
   ♥ 7 3
   ♦ Q 8 6 2
   ♣ J 9 7 3

b) ♠ 9 4
   ♥ 8 5
   ♦ A Q 10 7 6 3
   ♣ Q J 5

c) ♠ 9 7 6 2
   ♥ 6 2
   ♦ K Q 8
   ♣ Q 10 6 2

d) ♠ A 8 3
   ♥ Q J 5
   ♦ K J 6 2
   ♣ 10 8 5

e) ♠ K Q 9
   ♥ 10 4
   ♦ K 10 7 6
   ♣ Q J 5 2

f) ♠ J 7 3
   ♥ J 5 4
   ♦ Q 7 5
   ♣ Q 8 6 2

South opens 1♠ and North responds 1NT. What rebid would South make with each of the following hands?

WEST	NORTH	EAST	SOUTH
			1♠
PASS	1NT	PASS	?

g) ♠ A K J 5 4
   ♥ Q 8 7 3
   ♦ K 8
   ♣ 7 6

h) ♠ K Q 10 7 5
   ♥ A 9 3
   ♦ Q 4
   ♣ Q 9 5

i) ♠ A Q J 10 7 5
   ♥ K J
   ♦ A 9 3
   ♣ 7 2

j) ♠ A Q 8 7 5
   ♥ K 9
   ♦ A Q 8
   ♣ Q 10 6

k) ♠ A J 9 7 6 3
   ♥ 7
   ♦ A Q J 3 2
   ♣ 9

l) ♠ A K 9 7 3
   ♥ 6
   ♦ A 4
   ♣ A K 10 7 4

Answers to Quiz – Part II

a) **1NT**. With this hand, South makes the same response as in standard methods. The difference is that South's 1NT response is forcing. North must bid again, even if 1NT is actually the best contract!

b) **1NT**. With only 9 high-card points plus 2 length points for the six-card diamond suit, South isn't strong enough for a game-forcing 2♦ response. The good news is that opener will bid again, so South will have an opportunity to further describe the hand.

c) **1♠**. Responder's priority is to bid a four-card or longer spade suit rather than 1NT, even with a poor suit. Opener could have four spades, and the partnership doesn't want to miss its eight-card fit.

d) **1NT**. With 11 high-card points plus three-card support for hearts, responder starts with a forcing 1NT response, planning to jump to 3♥ at the next opportunity to show the fit and invitational strength.

e) **1NT**. With 11 high-card points, South is too strong to respond 1NT in standard methods. Playing 2/1, South starts with a forcing 1NT, planning to show extra strength at the next opportunity.

f) **1NT** (2♥). With three-card suppor, responder could raise immediately to 2♥. With such a poor hand, however, responder should take the more discouraging route of responding with a forcing 1NT, planning to simply give preference to hearts after opener's rebid.

g) **2♥**. After the 1NT response, South makes a natural rebid, showing the second suit, as in standard methods.

h) **2♣**. North's 1NT response is forcing, so South must find a rebid. Standard practice is to bid 2♣ with three cards in both minor suits.

i) **3♠**. With 15 high-card points plus 2 length points for the six-card suit, South can make a jump rebid to show a medium-strength opening.

j) **2NT**. 17 high-card points plus 1 length point for the five-card suit is too much to open 1NT. Raising to 2NT shows 18–19 points.

k) **2♦**. With 6-5 distribution, South starts with the six-card suit and then bids the five-card suit. South plans to rebid the diamonds if possible, showing at least a five-card diamond suit and five or more spades.

l) **3♣**. With 18 high-card points plus 1 length point for each five-card suit, South is too strong to rebid 2♣, which responder could pass. Instead South should make a game-forcing jump shift.

Quiz – Part III

North opens 1♠, South responds 1NT, and North rebids 2♦. What call does South make with each of the following hands?

WEST	NORTH	EAST	SOUTH	
	1♠	PASS	1NT	NORTH
PASS	2♦	PASS	?	WEST EAST
				SOUTH

a) ♠ 8 4
   ♥ Q 10 9 7 6 2
   ♦ 6 2
   ♣ A 7 5

b) ♠ 10 3
   ♥ K 8 6 2
   ♦ Q 9 5
   ♣ J 9 7 5

c) ♠ K 9 5
   ♥ Q J 7 2
   ♦ K 4
   ♣ Q 7 5 3

_____   _____   _____

d) ♠ J 4
   ♥ K Q 10 3
   ♦ Q 7 2
   ♣ Q J 9 5

e) ♠ 3
   ♥ J 9 5
   ♦ Q J 8 6
   ♣ K 8 7 6 3

f) ♠ 8 6
   ♥ A 9 5
   ♦ K J 7 5 3
   ♣ J 8 2

_____   _____   _____

What call does South make with the given hand in each of the following auctions?

g)

WEST	NORTH	EAST	SOUTH
			1♥
PASS	1NT	PASS	2♣
PASS	3♥	PASS	?

♠ Q J 7
♥ K 9 8 7 3
♦ K 6
♣ K 10 5

h)

WEST	NORTH	EAST	SOUTH
	PASS	PASS	1♠
PASS	1NT	PASS	?

♠ A Q J 7 2
♥ 9 3
♦ K J 8
♣ J 6 5

i)

WEST	NORTH	EAST	SOUTH
			1♥
1♠	1NT	PASS	?

♠ 9 4
♥ A Q 8 7 3
♦ K J 3
♣ K 8 6

Answers to Quiz – Part III

a) **2♥**. South wasn't strong enough to respond 2♥ immediately. Thanks to the forcing 1NT response, however, South can now show the heart suit without promising more than 6 points.

b) **2♠**. Although responder has more diamonds than spades, with a doubleton spade it's usually best to give preference back to opener's known five-card major. The partnership will be in at least a 5-2 fit. Opener's 2♦ rebid could be on a three-card suit, so it's best not to pass and risk playing in a 3-3 fit.

c) **3♠**. With 11 high-card points and three-card support for opener's major suit, South can show the values for an invitational raise by first responding with a forcing 1NT and then raising opener's suit to the three level.

d) **2NT**. With 11 high-card points and both unbid suits well stopped, South can make an invitational rebid of 2NT.

e) **Pass**. With a minimum response and a definite preference for diamonds, responder can pass opener's second suit. It's possible the partnership is in a 4-3 fit, but passing looks to be the best option.

f) **3♦**. With good support for opener's second suit, responder can make an invitational raise to the three level. With a minimum, opener will pass, but opener could have as many as 18 points, just short of a jump shift.

g) **Pass**. Responder's bid of a forcing 1NT followed by a jump raise to 3♥ shows three-card support for hearts and invitational values, about 11–12 points. With a minimum opening bid, South should pass, declining the invitation.

h) **Pass**. North passed originally, so the 1NT response is not forcing. With a minimum balanced hand, opener passes.

i) **Pass**. After West overcalls 1♠, North's 1NT bid is natural and non-forcing, showing about 6–10 points with at least one stopper in spades. With a minimum balanced hand, opener should leave partner in what is likely to be the best spot.

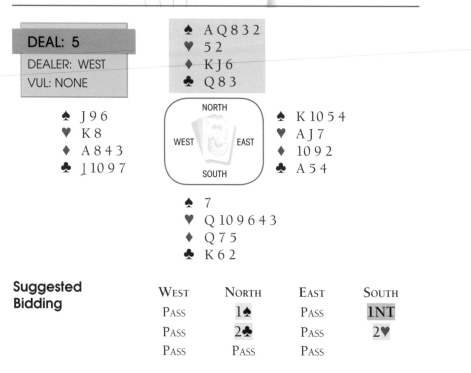

	DEAL: 5
	DEALER: WEST
	VUL: NONE

NORTH
♠ A Q 8 3 2
♥ 5 2
♦ K J 6
♣ Q 8 3

WEST
♠ J 9 6
♥ K 8
♦ A 8 4 3
♣ J 10 9 7

EAST
♠ K 10 5 4
♥ A J 7
♦ 10 9 2
♣ A 5 4

SOUTH
♠ 7
♥ Q 10 9 6 4 3
♦ Q 7 5
♣ K 6 2

Suggested Bidding

WEST	NORTH	EAST	SOUTH
PASS	1♠	PASS	1NT
PASS	2♣	PASS	2♥
PASS	PASS	PASS	

West passes. After North opens 1♠, South is not strong enough to respond 2♥, which would be game-forcing when playing 2/1. Instead, South makes a forcing 1NT response.

North cannot pass 1NT, since it is forcing. With no second suit to show and without a six-card major, North has to 'manufacture' a rebid. With a choice between two three-card minors, standard practice is to bid 2♣. This is similar to opening the bidding in a three-card minor suit.

Over the 2♣ rebid, South has the opportunity to show the heart suit. North can confidently pass the 2♥ bid. North 'knows' that South has a five-card or longer heart suit with too little strength to respond 2♥. The partnership reaches its best partscore.

Suggested Opening Lead

West leads the ♣J, top of the solid sequence.

Suggested Play

If declarer wins the first trick with the ♣K (see suggested defense), declarer should cross to dummy's ♠A and lead a heart and finesse the

♥9 if East plays low. Declarer has to lose the ♥A and ♥K, but avoids any more losers when East has the ♥J.

On the actual deal, the finesse succeeds and West has to win with the ♥K. On regaining the lead, declarer should lead a diamond to get to dummy and then lead the remaining heart from dummy, planning to repeat the finesse. Playing this way, declarer loses only two hearts, a diamond, and two clubs, making 2♥.

Suggested Defense

When West leads the ♣J and declarer plays a low club from dummy, East should play the ♣5, not the ♣A. If West has led top of an interior sequence and holds the ♣K, the ♣J will win the trick, so there's no need to play the ♣A. If South has the ♣K, playing the ♣A will give declarer two tricks in the suit, the ♣K and the ♣Q. Better to force declarer to win the first trick with the ♣K and keep the ♣Q trapped in dummy. This restricts declarer to the one club trick to which declarer is entitled, even if the ♣K is singleton. The defenders get two club tricks.

If declarer takes the heart finesse, the best the defenders can do is to hold declarer to eight tricks. If declarer chooses to take the spade finesse instead, the defenders can win a spade, two hearts, a diamond, and two clubs to defeat the contract.

Conclusion

In standard bidding, the auction might go:

WEST	NORTH	EAST	SOUTH
	1♠	PASS	1NT
PASS	PASS	PASS	

With a balanced minimum, North has no reason to bid over the non-forcing 1NT response. Unless East-West come into the auction, the partnership will miss the eight-card heart fit. South is unlikely to take seven tricks in a 1NT contract.

Using the forcing 1NT response, the partnership has a simple route to 2♥, the best contract.

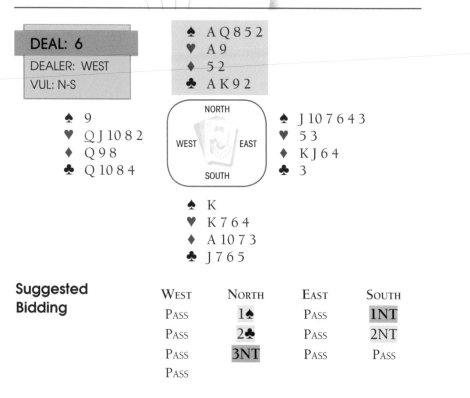

DEAL: 6

DEALER: WEST

VUL: N-S

♠ A Q 8 5 2
♥ A 9
♦ 5 2
♣ A K 9 2

NORTH

WEST   EAST

SOUTH

♠ 9
♥ Q J 10 8 2
♦ Q 9 8
♣ Q 10 8 4

♠ J 10 7 6 4 3
♥ 5 3
♦ K J 6 4
♣ 3

♠ K
♥ K 7 6 4
♦ A 10 7 3
♣ J 7 6 5

Suggested Bidding

WEST	NORTH	EAST	SOUTH
PASS	1♠	PASS	1NT
PASS	2♣	PASS	2NT
PASS	3NT	PASS	PASS
PASS			

With only 11 high-card points, South doesn't have enough strength for a 2/1 response to North's 1♠ opening. Instead, South settles for a forcing 1NT response. North makes the natural rebid in the club suit.

With 11 high-card points, South has enough to invite the partnership to game. A raise to 3♣ would be invitational, but South can't be certain that opener has a four-card suit. Opener might have bid a three-card suit with a balanced hand over the forcing 1NT. With stoppers in both hearts and diamonds, South can invite game by bidding 2NT, showing about 11–12 points. With less, South would pass 2♣, give preference to 2♠, or bid 2♦ or 2♥ with a long suit.

Holding 17 high-card points plus 1 length point for the five-card suit, North is happy to accept the invitation and take the partnership to game.

Suggested Opening Lead

West would lead the ♥Q, top of the solid sequence.

Suggested Play

Declarer has eight tricks: three sure spade tricks, two hearts, a diamond, and two clubs. Declarer could hope to develop an extra trick through length in the spade suit, hoping the seven missing spades are divided 4-3. However, the club suit offers a sure way to develop the extra trick.

Declarer can win the ♥K and take the ♠K to unblock the spade winners. Then declarer can play a club to dummy's ♣K and lead the ♣2 toward the ♣J. This is sure to succeed. If the five missing clubs are divided 3-2, declarer will always get an extra trick through length. If the clubs are divided 4-1 or 5-0 and East holds the ♣Q, South's ♣J will become a winner, whether or not East chooses to play the ♣Q.

On the actual deal, the clubs divide 4-1 and West has the ♣Q. That doesn't matter. South plays the ♣J and West wins the ♣Q. After regaining the lead, declarer comes to the South hand with the ♦A and leads a low club toward dummy's remaining ♣A-9. West's ♣10 is trapped and declarer has nine tricks.

The presence of the ♣9 in dummy makes this suit combination a sure thing for three tricks. Playing a high club and then leading toward the ♣J is a *safety play* to guarantee three tricks.

Suggested Defense

There is no defense to defeat 3NT if declarer handles the club suit correctly. If declarer plays the ♣A-K, however, the defenders can defeat the contract. Also, if South leads the ♣J, West should cover with the ♣Q[18].

Conclusion

In standard methods, the partnership might run into difficulties:

WEST	NORTH	EAST	SOUTH
	1♠	PASS	2♣
PASS	?		

With 11 high-card points, South is too strong to bid 1NT and might respond 2♣. Now North has a difficult choice of rebid and might jump to 4♣, getting the partnership past 3NT.

Starting with the forcing 1NT, the partnership can reach the best contract, 3NT.

---

[18] Declarer can still get an extra club trick by later leading to dummy's ♣9, but will need another entry to the South hand.

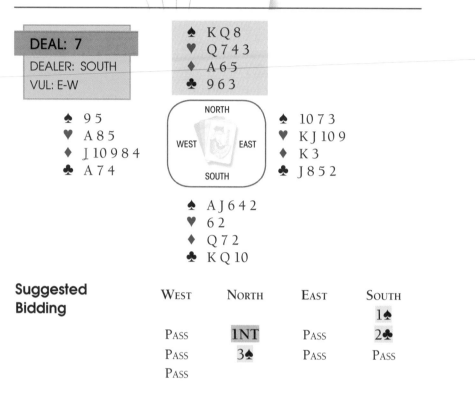

	♠ K Q 8	
	♥ Q 7 4 3	
DEAL: 7	♦ A 6 5	
DEALER: SOUTH	♣ 9 6 3	
VUL: E-W		

	NORTH	
♠ 9 5		♠ 10 7 3
♥ A 8 5	WEST EAST	♥ K J 10 9
♦ J 10 9 8 4		♦ K 3
♣ A 7 4	SOUTH	♣ J 8 5 2

	♠ A J 6 4 2
	♥ 6 2
	♦ Q 7 2
	♣ K Q 10

Suggested Bidding

WEST	NORTH	EAST	SOUTH
			1♠
PASS	1NT	PASS	2♣
PASS	3♠	PASS	PASS
PASS			

After South opens 1♠, North uses the forcing 1NT response to show a limit raise with three-card support. North starts with 1NT. With a minimum balanced hand, South can't pass. Instead, with a choice of two three-card minors, South bids 2♣. North jumps to 3♠, showing an invitational hand of 11–12 points with three-card support. With four-card support, North would have made a limit raise to 3♠ directly over 1♠.

South has a minimum hand with 12 high-card points plus 1 length point for the five-card spade suit. So South should reject the invitation, and the partnership stops in a partscore contract of 3♠.

Suggested Opening Lead

West will lead the ♦J, top of the solid sequence.

Suggested Play

Declarer has five sure spade tricks and a diamond. After the ♦J lead, South gets a trick with the ♦Q by playing low from dummy. If West has the ♦K, South's ♦Q will win; if East has the ♦K, the ♦Q will be a trick later.

So South needs two tricks from clubs. If East has the ♣A, South can try a repeated finesse by first leading a club from dummy to the ♣Q, and returning to dummy to lead another club toward the ♣K. If West has the ♣A, as on the actual deal, declarer can hope East has the ♣J and plan to take a finesse against it.

Suppose declarer plays a low diamond from dummy and East wins the ♦K and returns a diamond. South should win the ♦Q, keeping the ♦A as a later entry to dummy. South draws trumps by playing the ♠K, a low spade to the ♠J, and a spade to dummy's ♠Q. With trumps drawn, declarer is in the right hand to lead a low club toward the ♣K-Q. If West wins this trick with the ♣A (see below), declarer can use the ♦A as an entry to dummy to lead another club and finesse the ♣10, hoping East has the ♣J. The second finesse works, and declarer has nine tricks.

Suggested Defense

If declarer carefully uses dummy's entries to eventually finesse against East's ♣J, the defenders can't legitimately defeat 3♠. However, West can give declarer a tough guess by not winning the ♣A when declarer first leads a club from dummy to the ♣Q or ♣K. Declarer will probably assume East has the ♣A, and may cross back to dummy and lead a club to the remaining high honor. West wins this trick and the defenders will then get two club tricks to go with two hearts and a diamond. Great defense!

Conclusion

In standard bidding, the auction may start off more awkwardly:

West	North	East	South
			1♠
Pass	2♣?	Pass	3♣?
Pass	3♠	Pass	?

Over 1♠, North has too much to respond 1NT, but doesn't want to raise immediately to 3♠ since that would show four-card support. North can't respond 2♥ because that would promise a five-card suit. North will probably settle for 2♣. That gives South a difficult choice. South may not want to bid 2NT with nothing in hearts, and may choose to raise to 3♣. North can now show the spade support, and South can pass, but the auction goes far less smoothly than when using the forcing 1NT.

Using the forcing 1NT makes it easy to show a three-card limit raise.

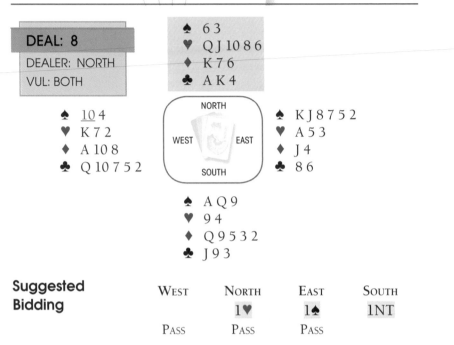

DEAL: 8

DEALER: NORTH
VUL: BOTH

NORTH
♠ 6 3
♥ Q J 10 8 6
♦ K 7 6
♣ A K 4

WEST
♠ 10 4
♥ K 7 2
♦ A 10 8
♣ Q 10 7 5 2

EAST
♠ K J 8 7 5 2
♥ A 5 3
♦ J 4
♣ 8 6

SOUTH
♠ A Q 9
♥ 9 4
♦ Q 9 5 3 2
♣ J 9 3

Suggested Bidding

WEST	NORTH	EAST	SOUTH
	1♥	1♠	1NT
PASS	PASS	PASS	

North opens 1♥. With a good six-card suit, East has enough to make a vulnerable overcall of 1♠. With stoppers in the opponent's spade suit and 9 high-card points plus 1 length point for the five-card diamond suit, South can respond 1NT to describe the hand. After interference from the opponents, South's 1NT bid is natural and invitational. It is not forcing.

With only two spades, West passes. North has a minimum, balanced hand with 13 high-card points plus 1 length point for the five-card heart suit. Since South's 1NT response is not forcing, North passes. Since East and West are vulnerable, East will likely pass as well, and the auction will finish at 1NT declared by South.

Suggested Opening Lead

West should lead the ♠10, top of the doubleton in partner's overcalled suit. It is usually best for partnership harmony to lead partner's suit unless there is clearly a better alternative.

Suggested Play

After the spade lead, declarer has two sure tricks in spades and two in clubs. The three additional tricks needed to make the contract can be promoted in the heart suit. So that's declarer's plan.

Since the opponents will have to be given the lead twice in hearts while promoting three winners in the suit, there is a danger that the defenders may be able to establish enough winners to defeat the contract. To make it more difficult for the defenders to establish spade winners, South should let the defenders win the first spade trick. See below what might happen if declarer wins the first spade.

Suppose declarer lets West win the first trick with the ♠10, and West leads another spade. Declarer wins this trick and leads a heart. If West wins the ♥K, West doesn't have a spade left to lead. Declarer wins whatever suit West returns and drives out East's ♥A while still having a stopper in the spade suit. If East wins the first heart trick with the ♥A and leads another spade to drive out declarer's remaining high card, that's also okay. When declarer leads another heart, West can win the ♥K, but has no entry to North's established spade winners. Declarer wins the race to establish tricks[19].

Suggested Defense

Suppose declarer wins the first spade trick with the ♠Q as East makes an encouraging signal with the ♠8. When declarer leads a heart, West can defeat the contract by immediately winning the ♥K and leading the ♠4. Even if South holds up the ♠A, East can continue the suit to drive it out. Now when East wins a trick with the ♥A, East can take the remaining spade winners and then lead a diamond to West's ♦A. The defenders get four spade tricks, two hearts, and a diamond.

It may seem strange for West to play second hand high when a heart is led, but West wants to preserve East's hoped-for entry, the ♥A, until the spades are established. This would be an excellent defensive play by West if declarer doesn't hold up winning the first round of spades.

Conclusion

Once East overcalls 1♠, the partnership goes back to standard methods. South's 1NT response is not forcing and shows 6–10 points plus a spade stopper.

The forcing 1NT no longer applies once an opponent interferes over the opening bid.

---

[19] If both defenders let declarer win the first round of hearts, declarer can still make the contract.

The fact that the partnership is committed to game influences opener's choice of rebids in some, but not all, situations. The primary difference between opener's rebids playing the two-over-one system and playing Standard methods is that, after responder's two-over-one bid, there is no longer the necessity to jump the bidding with a strong hand.

—STEVE BRUNO AND MAX HARDY
Two-Over-One Game Force:
An Introduction (1993)

Rebids by Opener
and Responder After 2/1

A big advantage of 2/1 Game Force is that it relieves the pressure on opener and responder to be concerned about both How High and Where at the same time. How High has already been partially answered: at least game. So both opener and responder can focus on Where when choosing their rebid. Whether the partnership belongs in slam can be investigated once Where has been resolved.

Focus on Where

Once an eight-card or longer major suit fit is found, there is rarely a need to consider another suit[20]. So if either player raises partner's major suit, the trump suit is agreed, the rest of the auction can focus on whether there is enough extra strength for slam. Subsequent bids in another suit are slam investigations, as will be discussed in Chapter 4.

The situation is not as clear-cut when the partnership has found an eight-card or longer minor-suit fit. Unless the partnership has enough extra strength to consider slam in the minor suit, the option of playing game in 3NT is still a possibility. So raising partner's minor suit does not necessarily settle the issue of Where. Subsequent bids below the game level can be ambiguous. They may be attempts to reach 3NT, or they may be the prelude to a slam investigation. Until it becomes clear, it is best to assume that the partnership is still searching for the best game.

---

[20] There are exceptions. Sometimes the partnership can make nine tricks in notrump but not ten in a major suit fit; sometimes more tricks can be made in a 4-4 fit in another suit. However, these exceptions are best ignored for now.

Opener's Rebid[21]

When choosing a rebid, opener's focus is on describing the shape of the hand. Opener's priorities are to:

- Support responder's suit.
- Bid a second suit.
- Rebid a six-card or longer suit.
- Bid notrump.

SUPPORTING RESPONDER'S MAJOR

The only time responder makes a 2/1 response in a major is when the opening bid is 1♠ and responder bids 2♥[22].

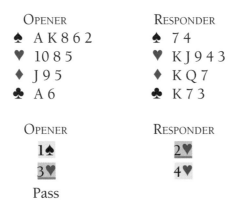

OPENER	RESPONDER
♠ A K 8 6 2	♠ 7 4
♥ 10 8 5	♥ K J 9 4 3
♦ J 9 5	♦ K Q 7
♣ A 6	♣ K 7 3

OPENER	RESPONDER
1♠	2♥
3♥	4♥
Pass	

Since the 2♥ response promises a five-card or longer suit, opener needs only three-card support to raise and agree on the trump suit. Even with a balanced hand, opener's priority is to support the major suit. Once the eight-card major suit fit is found and neither partner has enough to consider a slam, the partnership settles into the major-suit game.

---

[21] Jump rebids by opener are discussed in Appendix 7.

[22] After a 1♥ opening, for example, responder's 1♠ bid is not a 2/1 Game Force.

This next example illustrates good use of the extra bidding space to avoid reaching a poor slam.

OPENER	RESPONDER
♠ K Q J 7 3	♠ A 4
♥ A J 4 2	♥ K Q 10 8 7
♦ J 6	♦ 8 3
♣ A 9	♣ K Q J 4

OPENER	RESPONDER
1♠	2♥
3♥	3♠
4♣	4♥
Pass	

Here opener has a medium-strength opening bid, but opener doesn't need to jump to show the extra strength. The priority is to simply agree on the trump suit, leaving room to explore for slam. Both partners have some extra strength, but it takes a delicate auction to discover there is no slam, because the opponents can take the first two diamond tricks. Responder shows a control in spades, the ♠A, and opener shows the ♣A. But neither partner can show a control in the diamond suit. Slam exploration is covered in more detail in the next chapter, but the point is that after the 2/1 response, the partnership doesn't want to unnecessarily use up additional bidding room while agreeing on where to play.

SUPPORTING RESPONDER'S MINOR

Responder doesn't guarantee a five-card suit for a response of 2♣ or 2♦, and game in a minor suit is usually less attractive than game in notrump. So four-card support is normally required to raise responder's minor, although opener can raise with strong three-card support.

OPENER	RESPONDER
♠ 7 4	♠ A J 10
♥ A J 8 5 2	♥ 10 4
♦ Q 6	♦ K 10 3
♣ A Q 8 3	♣ K J 7 6 2

OPENER	RESPONDER
1♥	2♣
3♣	3NT
Pass	

With four-card support for responder's minor, opener raises to 3♣. Although the partnership has uncovered a nine-card minor-suit fit, responder suggests playing game in notrump with a balanced hand and nothing extra. Having already shown the heart suit and club support, opener accepts responder's decision.

OPENER	RESPONDER
♠ 8 6	♠ A K 3
♥ A K 10 6 3	♥ J 4
♦ A Q 10	♦ K J 8 7 5
♣ 9 4 3	♣ A Q 5

OPENER	RESPONDER
1♥	2♦
3♦	4NT
5♥	5NT
6♦	Pass

Opener has strong three-card support for responder's minor, with all the high cards concentrated in hearts and diamonds. Opener's raise to 3♦ encourages responder to continue to the excellent slam.

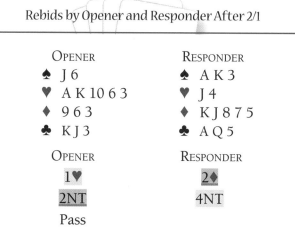

OPENER	RESPONDER
♠ J 6	♠ A K 3
♥ A K 10 6 3	♥ J 4
♦ 9 6 3	♦ K J 8 7 5
♣ K J 3	♣ A Q 5

OPENER	RESPONDER
1♥	2♦
2NT	4NT
Pass	

Here opener has poor three-card support for responder's minor, and the high cards are located in other suits. Opener chooses 2NT as the most descriptive rebid. This will slow responder down. Responder makes a slam-invitational raise to 4NT, but opener passes and the partnership stops safely in a game contract.

SHOWING A SECOND SUIT

Opener **always** shows a second five-card suit. Opener shows a four-card suit **except** with a minimum hand when the suit would have to be bid at the three level.

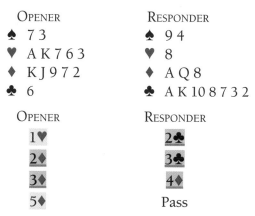

OPENER	RESPONDER
♠ 7 3	♠ 9 4
♥ A K 7 6 3	♥ 8
♦ K J 9 7 2	♦ A Q 8
♣ 6	♣ A K 10 8 7 3 2

OPENER	RESPONDER
1♥	2♣
2♦	3♣
3♦	4♦
5♦	Pass

Opener shows the diamonds over the game-forcing 2♣ response, and rebids the suit to show at least 5-5 distribution. Responder then raises diamonds, and the partnership reaches 5♦, avoiding 3NT where the defenders will likely take at least five spade tricks.

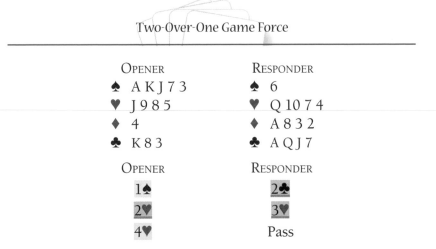

OPENER	RESPONDER
♠ A K J 7 3	♠ 6
♥ J 9 8 5	♥ Q 10 7 4
♦ 4	♦ A 8 3 2
♣ K 8 3	♣ A Q J 7

OPENER	RESPONDER
1♠	2♣
2♥	3♥
4♥	Pass

Over the 1♠ opening, responder can't bid 2♥ since that would promise a five-card or longer suit. So responder starts with 2♣. Although opener has good support for clubs, the priority is to show a four-card heart suit whenever possible, otherwise the fit might be lost. Responder raises to 3♥ to agree on trumps. With a minimum opening and a poor heart suit, opener settles for game[23].

OPENER	RESPONDER
♠ A Q 8 3	♠ 6 5 2
♥ A Q 9 5 4	♥ 8 3
♦ 7 4	♦ K Q J 10 8
♣ 9 3	♣ A Q 5

OPENER	RESPONDER
1♥	2♦
2♠	2NT
3NT	Pass

Opener would have an awkward choice of rebid over 2♦ in standard methods since a 2♠ rebid would be a *reverse*, promising extra values. Opener would likely rebid 2♥ to show a minimum hand. Not a very descriptive rebid. Playing 2/1, opener can rebid 2♠.

---

[23] Opener might try for slam by bidding 4♣ to show the club control, and responder might make a control-showing bid of 4♦. However, neither player has quite enough to take the partnership beyond game.

A new suit at the two level doesn't promise any extra strength, even when it is higher-ranking than opener's first suit[24]. The partnership is already committed to at least the game level. The descriptive rebid gives the partnership an easy time reaching 3NT, the best contract.

OPENER	RESPONDER
♠ 10 4	♠ K Q 9
♥ A Q 8 5 4 3	♥ 6
♦ K Q 10 2	♦ J 7 3
♣ 3	♣ A K Q 8 5 2

OPENER	RESPONDER
1♥	2♣
2♦	3♣
3♥	3NT
Pass	Pass

With 6-4 distribution, opener usually shows the four-card suit in preference to rebidding the six-card suit, unless the four-card suit is very weak or cannot be shown at the two level. Opener plans to rebid the six-card suit at the next opportunity, as in the above auction. This is sometimes referred to as the '6-4-6' approach: six-card suit, then four-card suit, then rebid the six-card suit.

Showing the four-card suit is generally more descriptive than rebidding the six-card suit. In the above auction, responder already knows opener has at least five hearts. A rebid of 2♥ would show only one additional card, the sixth heart. Bidding 2♦ lets responder know about nine cards in opener's hand: at least five hearts and four diamonds. There's no hurry to show the extra length in hearts. Since the partnership is forced to game, opener will have an opportunity to show the extra length later.

---

[24] Some partnerships prefer that opener's reverse still promises a bit extra when playing 2/1, but the popular approach is that it simply describes opener's shape, nothing more.

Of course, there are always exceptions:

OPENER	RESPONDER
♠ K Q J 10 8 5	♠ 9 3
♥ A 4	♥ J 7
♦ 9 8 6 3	♦ A 10 7 5
♣ J	♣ A K 8 7 5

OPENER	RESPONDER
1♠	2♣
2♠	3♠
4♠	Pass

With a minimum opening bid, opener elects to rebid the good six-card spade suit rather than introducing the weak four-card diamond suit. The partnership reaches 4♠, which is a reasonable contract. 5♦ would have no chance, since declarer would have to lose at least a spade trick and two diamonds.

Opener's bid of a new suit at the three level shows either:

- Extra distribution—a five-card suit—**or**
- Extra strength—about 15 or more high-card points.

Opener	Responder
♠ A K 9 7 6	♠ 4
♥ 2	♥ A Q 9 6 3
♦ K J 10 5 3	♦ Q 9 8 2
♣ 7 2	♣ A 4 3

Opener	Responder
1♠	2♥
3♦	4♦
5♦	Pass

Opener is willing to show the five-card diamond suit at the three level, even with a minimum hand. Responder, expecting either extra strength or extra distribution, is willing to go past 3NT and show the diamond support. 5♦ is a better contract than 3NT on these combined hands.

Opener	Responder
♠ A K 9 7 6	♠ 4
♥ 2	♥ A Q 9 6 3
♦ K J 10 5	♦ Q 9 8 2
♣ K Q 2	♣ A 4 3

Opener	Responder
1♠	2♥
3♦	4♦
4NT	5♥
6♦	Pass

Here opener has extra strength and is willing to go to the three level to show the diamonds, even with a four-card suit. Once the fit is found, opener uses Blackwood to check that the partnership isn't missing two aces, and goes for the slam bonus.

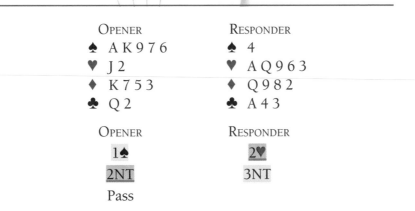

OPENER	RESPONDER
♠ A K 9 7 6	♠ 4
♥ J 2	♥ A Q 9 6 3
♦ K 7 5 3	♦ Q 9 8 2
♣ Q 2	♣ A 4 3

OPENER	RESPONDER
1♠	2♥
2NT	3NT
Pass	

With a minimum hand, opener is unwilling to go to the three level to show the four-card diamond suit, and chooses to treat the hand as balanced by rebidding 2NT. The partnership may miss the diamond fit on this deal, but that's not so bad. Although it may be challenging to find nine tricks in 3NT, that's a lot better than trying to find eleven tricks in 5♦.

SHOWING A SIX-CARD OR LONGER SUIT

Opener's rebid of the original suit over the 2/1 response generally shows a six-card or longer suit.

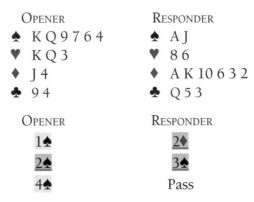

OPENER	RESPONDER
♠ K Q 9 7 6 4	♠ A J
♥ K Q 3	♥ 8 6
♦ J 4	♦ A K 10 6 3 2
♣ 9 4	♣ Q 5 3

OPENER	RESPONDER
1♠	2♦
2♠	3♠
4♠	Pass

With a six-card suit and a minimum hand, opener simply rebids the spades. Responder can raise spades to agree on the trump suit, knowing the partnership has an eight-card major suit fit. With nothing extra, opener settles for game.

There's no need for opener to jump to show extra strength:

OPENER	RESPONDER
♠ K Q 9 7 6 4	♠ A J
♥ A K J	♥ 8 6
♦ J 4	♦ A K 10 6 3 2
♣ K 9	♣ Q 5 3

OPENER	RESPONDER
1♠	2♦
2♠	3♠
4NT	5♥
6♠	Pass

With considerable extra values, opener still rebids only 2♠. The priority is to show the extra length. The extra strength can wait until a fit has been found. Once responder shows the support for spades, opener can launch into Blackwood and bid the excellent slam when the partnership is missing only one ace.

SHOWING A BALANCED HAND

After a 2/1 response, opener shows a balanced hand with a rebid of 2NT.

OPENER	RESPONDER
♠ K 9 4	♠ Q J 3
♥ A J 8 5 3	♥ 7 2
♦ K 8 2	♦ A Q 5
♣ J 3	♣ K Q 10 5 2

OPENER	RESPONDER
1♥	2♣
2NT	3NT
Pass	

With a minimum balanced hand of 12 high-card points plus 1 length point for the five-card heart suit, opener makes the descriptive rebid of 2NT. Responder is comfortable settling for game in notrump.

Opener won't have a balanced hand of 15–17 points for the 2NT rebid, since that type of hand would have been opened 1NT. However, opener could either have a balanced hand of about 12–14 points, too weak to open 1NT, or a balanced hand of about 18-19 points, too strong to open 1NT. For example:

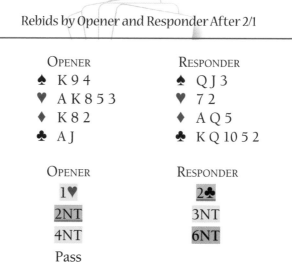

Opener	Responder
♠ K 9 4	♠ Q J 3
♥ A K 8 5 3	♥ 7 2
♦ K 8 2	♦ A Q 5
♣ A J	♣ K Q 10 5 2

Opener	Responder
1♥	2♣
2NT	3NT
4NT	6NT
Pass	

Here opener has 18 high-card points plus 1 length point for the five-card heart suit. Over the 2♣ response, there's no need to jump to 3NT, since the 2NT rebid is forcing to game. So opener starts by describing the shape of the hand, not the strength. After responder agrees to play in notrump, opener shows extra strength by making an invitational—*quantitative*—raise to 4NT. Responder, with more than a bare minimum, accepts the invitation, and the partnership reaches slam.

Opener will not always be perfectly balanced for a rebid of 2NT. With a minimum opening bid, it might be the most descriptive call opener can make. For example:

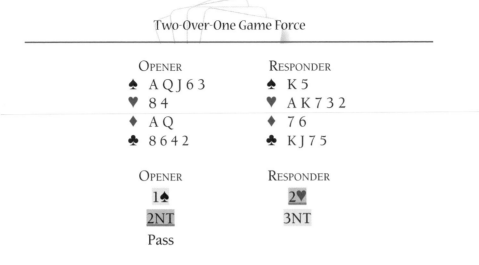

OPENER	RESPONDER
♠ A Q J 6 3	♠ K 5
♥ 8 4	♥ A K 7 3 2
♦ A Q	♦ 7 6
♣ 8 6 4 2	♣ K J 7 5

OPENER	RESPONDER
1♠	2♥
2NT	3NT
Pass	

With a minimum, opener isn't strong enough to show the weak second suit at the three level, which would promise either extra strength or extra distribution. Instead, opener rebids 2NT, and responder simply raises to game. If opener had bid 3♣, responder would probably raise to 4♣, and the partnership might get overboard.

OPENER	RESPONDER
♠ A J 8 6 3	♠ 7 2
♥ K 9 3	♥ 8 5
♦ 4	♦ A K Q J 5
♣ K J 7 5	♣ A 6 4 2

OPENER	RESPONDER
1♠	2♦
2NT	3NT
Pass	

Here opener is even more unbalanced. However, after the 2♦ response, opener isn't strong enough to introduce the club suit at the three level. A rebid of 2NT is the most descriptive rebid opener can make, and responder will be happy to settle for game. Again, if opener shows the club suit, responder will be tempted to raise, and the partnership will beyond its best spot.

STOPPERS

Does opener need *stoppers* (see box) in the unbid suits to bid 2NT? Although some authorities insist that opener have a stopper in any unbid suit to rebid 2NT, the recommended approach is that opener's 2NT rebid doesn't guarantee a stopper in the unbid suits.

OPENER	RESPONDER
♠ A 10 5 4 3	♠ 8 2
♥ A K 3	♥ Q J 2
♦ 10 7 3	♦ J 4 2
♣ Q 2	♣ A K J 7 5

OPENER	RESPONDER
1♠	2♣
2NT	3NT
Pass	

With a minimum balanced hand, opener has to find a rebid after 2♣. Opener can't support clubs with a doubleton; opener can't bid a new suit with only three cards[25]; a 2♠ rebid would show a six-card suit. So the most descriptive rebid is 2NT. The partnership reaches 3NT when neither player has a diamond stopper. Still, 3NT is the best contract. The defenders may not lead a diamond, the missing diamonds might divide 4-3, or the suit might be *blocked*.

WHAT IS A STOPPER?

A *stopper* is a value that will, or likely will, stop the opponents from taking all the tricks in a suit they lead.

An Ace is obviously a stopper, as is K-Q or Q-J-10. Since the opening lead comes around to declarer's hand, a holding such as Q-J-2 would also be a stopper.

A holding such as K-2 in declarer's hand, will be a stopper if the suit is led from declarer's left. It will be a *potential* stopper if it is in the dummy, since the ace could be favorably located.

Holdings such as Q-2, J-3-2, or 10-7-5-4, are called a ½ stopper. If partner has a similar holding, the partnership has a full stopper.

---

[25] Opener can bid a three-card minor in some situations, such as after a forcing 1NT response, but not here.

Responder's Rebid[26]

When it is time for responder to make a rebid, opener has bid twice, providing a good description of opener's hand. Responder will usually be able to decide **WHERE** the partnership belongs. Any bid by responder below the game level is still forcing, so there's no need to jump to game if there is uncertainty about the best contract. Responder's options are:

* Agree on a trump suit if that hasn't happened already.
* Rebid a six-card or longer suit.
* Suggest notrump if there is no major-suit fit.
* Bid the fourth suit to get more information from opener.

AGREEING ON A TRUMP SUIT

Once the partnership can agree on a major suit, the only remaining decision will be whether to move toward slam.

OPENER	RESPONDER
♠ Q 10 8 7 6 3	♠ J 9 4
♥ J 4	♥ K Q 8 6 5
♦ K J	♦ A 9 3
♣ K J 2	♣ A 3

OPENER	RESPONDER
1♠	2♥
2♠	3♠
4♠	Pass

Once responder raises spades, the trump suit has been agreed. With nothing extra, opener simply bids game. Responder has nothing more to say.

---

[26] Jump rebids by responder are discussed in Appendix 7.

OPENER	RESPONDER
♠ K Q 10 7 5	♠ 6 2
♥ A J 8 3	♥ K Q 9 2
♦ Q 8	♦ A J 10 7 3
♣ 7 4	♣ A 8

OPENER	RESPONDER
1♠	2♦
2♥	3♥
4♥	Pass

Here responder has support for opener's second suit, hearts, and shows this by raising to the three level. Responder must have at least four-card support to raise opener's second suit. Responder doesn't have to jump to game, since 3♥ is still forcing. Responder has a little extra, and there might be a slam. However, when opener makes no move toward slam, responder settles for game.

If opener has raised responder's minor suit, it is still possible that the partnership belongs in a major suit or notrump.

OPENER	RESPONDER
♠ A Q 10 7 5	♠ K 9 3
♥ 6 2	♥ Q 3
♦ K Q 8 5	♦ A J 9 7 3
♣ J 8	♣ A 6 5

OPENER	RESPONDER
1♠	2♦
3♦	3♠
4♠	Pass

With enough strength to take the partnership to game, but only three-card support for opener's major, responder starts with a new suit. Even though opener shows support for diamonds, responder follows through by showing support for the major suit. 4♠ is a much better contract than 5♦, since there are three top losers: the ♠A, and ♥A-K.

REBIDDING A SUIT

If opener hasn't raised responder's suit, responder can bid it again to show a six-card or longer suit.

Opener	Responder
♠ A Q 8 5 2	♠ 4 3
♥ 10 2	♥ A Q J 8 4 3
♦ A J 5	♦ K Q 8
♣ Q 8 2	♣ 7 5

Opener	Responder
1♠	2♥
2NT	3♥
4♥	Pass

After opener rebids 2NT to show a balanced hand, responder rebids the heart suit to show the extra length. Opener now knows there is an eight-card major-suit fit and takes the partnership to the best game contract.

Opener	Responder
♠ Q J 8 7 2	♠ 6
♥ A 9 8 5	♥ K J 3
♦ K Q 9	♦ 10 3
♣ 4	♣ A K J 10 8 7 5

Opener	Responder
1♠	2♣
2♥	3♣
3NT	Pass

After opener rebids 2♥, responder can simply rebid the club suit to show the extra length. There's no need to jump to game, since the 3♣ bid is forcing. This would give opener a chance to rebid the hearts with a five-card suit. On the actual hand, opener can bid game in notrump with a diamond stopper. Responder comfortably passes, having already described the hand.

SUGGESTING NOTRUMP

If the partnership doesn't appear to have a major-suit fit, responder can suggest playing in notrump, even if the partnership has found a minor-suit fit. Nine tricks are usually easier than eleven.

OPENER	RESPONDER
♠ A J 9 8 5 3	♠ 4
♥ K 4	♥ A 10 9 2
♦ K 5	♦ A Q J 8 3
♣ J 7 2	♣ Q 9 4

OPENER	RESPONDER
1♠	2♦
2♠	2NT
3NT	Pass

Opener's priority is to rebid the spade suit to show the extra length. With no fit for spades, responder suggests playing the contract in notrump. There's no point in showing the heart suit to look for a fit. Opener would have bid 2♥ rather than 2♠, holding four or more hearts. Opener is happy to accept responder's choice of notrump, having already shown the six-card spade suit.

OPENER	RESPONDER
♠ 6 4	♠ Q J 2
♥ A Q 9 8 5	♥ 4
♦ 10 2	♦ A J 3
♣ A Q 8 3	♣ K J 9 7 5 2

OPENER	RESPONDER
1♥	2♣
3♣	3NT
Pass	

Here opener raises responder's minor and the partnership finds its club fit. However, responder doesn't want to bypass 3NT holding stoppers in both the unbid suits. Opener has already shown the heart suit and the club support, so there's no reason to override responder's suggestion.

When the partnership has bid three suits, responder should have a stopper in the unbid suit to suggest playing in notrump.

OPENER	RESPONDER
♠ 7 3	♠ K 8
♥ A J 8 6 5	♥ 7 4
♦ Q 4	♦ A K J 8 7 3
♣ A K J 8	♣ 9 4 2

OPENER	RESPONDER
1♥	2♦
3♣	3NT
Pass	

With a spade stopper, responder suggests playing in 3NT. That's the best contract for the partnership.

Why does responder need a stopper to suggest notrump while opener can rebid 2NT without worrying about stoppers in the unbid suits? The difference is that there are **two** unbid suits when opener rebids 2NT after a 2/1 response. It's too restrictive to make opener responsible for stoppers in both suits. It's also unclear which of the two suits the defenders will lead. The defender on opening lead may not lead the suit in which opener has no stopper; or responder might have a stopper in that suit anyway.

When there is only **one** unbid suit, it becomes pretty clear which suit the defenders are likely to lead. So it makes sense to have a stopper in that suit to bid notrump. There is also positional value in having the player holding the stopper being declarer. In the above deal, it is very likely the opponents will lead a spade, the one suit that opener and responder have not bid. It's a good idea for responder to bid 3NT, because the lead will then be coming from the opponent to responder's left. If the opponents lead a spade, responder is sure to get a trick with the ♠K. If opener were declarer in 3NT and responder's hand were the dummy, an opening spade lead would put the contract in danger if the ♠A is unfavorably placed.

BIDDING FOURTH SUIT

In standard methods, responder often needs to find a forcing rebid to get more information from opener to help decide How High and Where the partnership belongs. Since responder's bid of an *old* suit—a suit previously bid by the partnership—is not forcing in many auctions, most partnerships use responder's bid of the fourth suit as an artificial game-forcing bid. When playing 2/1 Game Force, however, there is no need to use fourth suit this way, since the partnership is already commited to game after a 2/1 response. Instead, fourth suit takes on one of two meanings:

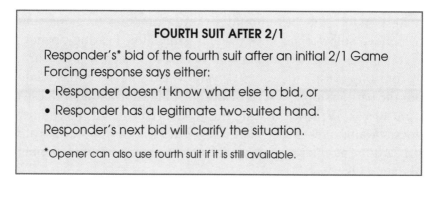

FOURTH SUIT AFTER 2/1

Responder's* bid of the fourth suit after an initial 2/1 Game Forcing response says either:

- Responder doesn't know what else to bid, or
- Responder has a legitimate two-suited hand.

Responder's next bid will clarify the situation.

*Opener can also use fourth suit if it is still available.

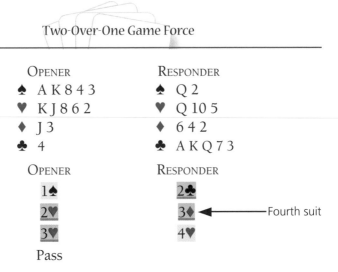

OPENER	RESPONDER
♠ A K 8 4 3	♠ Q 2
♥ K J 8 6 2	♥ Q 10 5
♦ J 3	♦ 6 4 2
♣ 4	♣ A K Q 7 3

OPENER	RESPONDER
1♠	2♣
2♥	3♦ ◄——— Fourth suit
3♥	4♥
Pass	

Responder's 2♣ bid commits the partnership to game, but responder still doesn't know which game after hearing opener's first two bids. The partnership may belong in spades, hearts, clubs, or notrump. Responder doesn't want to bid 2♠, since that might put the partnership in a seven-card fit. Similarly, responder doesn't want to bid 3♥, since that might be a seven-card fit. Responder doesn't want to rebid 3♣, since that would tend to show a six-card suit. And responder doesn't want to bid notrump with no stopper in diamonds.

So responder bids 3♦ as a 'punt'—"I don't know what else to do." Once opener rebids hearts, responder knows exactly what to do.

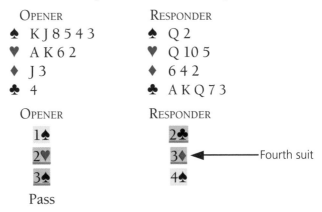

OPENER	RESPONDER
♠ K J 8 5 4 3	♠ Q 2
♥ A K 6 2	♥ Q 10 5
♦ J 3	♦ 6 4 2
♣ 4	♣ A K Q 7 3

OPENER	RESPONDER
1♠	2♣
2♥	3♦ ◄——— Fourth suit
3♠	4♠
Pass	

This time opener shows the extra length in spades, and responder is now happy to raise to game.

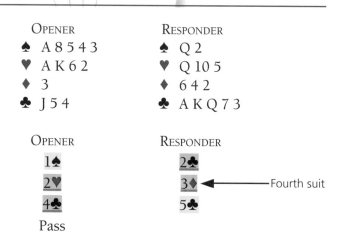

OPENER	RESPONDER
♠ A 8 5 4 3	♠ Q 2
♥ A K 6 2	♥ Q 10 5
♦ 3	♦ 6 4 2
♣ J 5 4	♣ A K Q 7 3

OPENER	RESPONDER	
1♠	2♣	
2♥	3♦	◄———— Fourth suit
4♣	5♣	
Pass		

Here opener shows the club support, and the partnership once again lands in the best contract. Opener avoids bidding 3NT because 3♦ doesn't promise anything in diamonds; responder could have bid 2NT with a diamond stopper.

OPENER	RESPONDER
♠ K 8 5 4 3	♠ Q 2
♥ A K 6 2	♥ Q 10 5
♦ K 3	♦ 6 4 2
♣ J 4	♣ A K Q 7 3

OPENER	RESPONDER	
1♠	2♣	
2♥	3♦	◄———— Fourth suit
3NT	Pass	

With a stopper in the fourth suit—diamonds in this case—opener is expected to bid notrump with no other special feature to show. This is often exactly what responder is hoping opener will do.

After all, responder could bid notrump with some values in the fourth suit. For example:

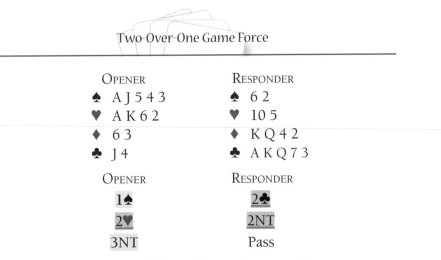

OPENER	RESPONDER
♠ A J 5 4 3	♠ 6 2
♥ A K 6 2	♥ 10 5
♦ 6 3	♦ K Q 4 2
♣ J 4	♣ A K Q 7 3

OPENER	RESPONDER
1♠	2♣
2♥	2NT
3NT	Pass

With stoppers in the unbid suit, diamonds, responder can suggest a notrump contract instead of bidding the fourth suit. With such moderate values, there is little value in bidding 3♦ as a natural suit. Opener has shown length in hearts and spades, so notrump is probably best.

With a two-suited hand unsuitable for playing in 3NT, responder clarifies the situation on the next round. For example:

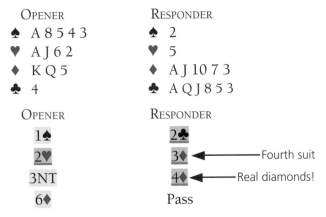

OPENER	RESPONDER
♠ A 8 5 4 3	♠ 2
♥ A J 6 2	♥ 5
♦ K Q 5	♦ A J 10 7 3
♣ 4	♣ A Q J 8 5 3

OPENER	RESPONDER	
1♠	2♣	
2♥	3♦	◄——Fourth suit
3NT	4♦	◄——Real diamonds!
6♦	Pass	

After responder bids the fourth suit, opener assumes partner is simply looking for the best place to play and bids 3NT to show the stopper in diamonds. Now responder rebids the diamonds to show a real two-suited hand. Opener has excellent values opposite responder's expected distribution and will likely take the partnership to slam. Opener might make a control-showing bid or use Blackwood, but a jump to slam gets the partnership to a reasonable spot. More on slam bidding in the next chapter.

Responder isn't the only one who can use fourth suit with nothing better to do. In some auctions, opener has fourth suit available.

OPENER	RESPONDER
♠ 6 4	♠ K 3
♥ A Q J 7 5	♥ 3
♦ K Q 9 2	♦ 6 5 3
♣ 10 5	♣ A K Q 8 7 6 2

OPENER	RESPONDER
1♥	2♣
2♦	3♣
Fourth suit ⟶ 3♠	3NT
Pass	

After responder rebids clubs, opener has to decide what to do. With no stopper in the unbid suit, spades, and having already shown hearts and diamonds, opener bids 3♠ as fourth suit. With a spade stopper, responder is comfortable bidding 3NT, and the partnership plays 3NT from the best side. If opener were declarer, a spade lead would defeat the contract if the ♠A is unfavorably located.

OPENER	RESPONDER
♠ 6 4	♠ 3 2
♥ A Q J 7 5	♥ K 3
♦ K Q 9 2	♦ 6 5 4
♣ 10 5	♣ A K Q 8 7 6

OPENER	RESPONDER
1♥	2♣
2♦	3♣
Fourth suit ⟶ 3♠	4♥
Pass	

Here, opener again uses fourth suit with nothing else to say. With no stopper in spades, responder suggests playing in hearts. Since responder would have shown three-card heart support on the previous round, instead of rebidding 3♣, opener is aware that responder has only two. However, with neither partner having anything in spades, it seems that 4♥ is the best spot, even on a 5-2 fit. And indeed it is! The defenders can get only two spades and the ♦A.

When the Opponents Interfere

If there is interference directly over the opening bid, 2/1 Game Force is off. However, if either opponent enters the auction after the initial 2/1 response, the game force is still on, although doubling the opponents becomes an alternative to continuing on to game.

Both opener and responder can continue to bid naturally, but they are presented with three additional options:

- Pass
- Double
- Cuebid the opponent's suit (rare)[27]

PASSING

If the opponent's bid makes it inconvenient to find a suitable rebid, pass is an option. Since the partnership is already committed to game, a pass is forcing. Partner is expected to keep the auction going.

WEST	NORTH	EAST	SOUTH	
			1♥	
Pass	2♣	2♠	?	

♠ J 5 4
♥ K Q 10 8 3
♦ A Q 4
♣ J 6

Pass. If East had passed, South would rebid 2NT to show the balanced hand. When East overcalls 2♠, South doesn't have to bid 2NT with no real spade stopper. Instead, South can pass, saying: "I've got nothing particular to say at this point. Over to you, partner!" The auction won't end in 2♠, since North's 2♣ response is still forcing to game.

---

[27] Cuebids can have many meanings, depending on the situation and the partnership agreements. Most are outside the scope of this book. When an opponent interferes in a 2/1 auction, a cuebid of the opponent's suit typically shows support for partner's suit and interest in slam. Slam bidding is discussed in more detail in Chapter 4.

WEST	NORTH	EAST	SOUTH
	1♠	Pass	2♣
2♦	2♥	3♦	?

```
        NORTH
  WEST         EAST
        SOUTH
```

♠ K 4
♥ Q 6 2
♦ 8 7
♣ A Q J 8 4 2

Pass. If East had passed, South could rebid 3♣ to show the extra length in clubs and hear what opener has to say next. Over East's 3♦ bid, South would have to bid 4♣ to show the sixth club. That would take the partnership beyond 3NT, and there's no guarantee North has any fit for clubs. After all, North bid spades and hearts. South can simply pass, waiting to hear what opener has to say next. North might rebid 3♥, which South can raise to 4♥; or North might bid 3NT, which South would be content to pass. Or North might do something else. It doesn't matter. The key point is that South's pass is forcing since game has not yet been reached.

DOUBLING

Although the partnership is 'committed to game' after a 2/1 response, it doesn't necessarily have to bid to game! If the opponents interfere, the partnership can choose to double for penalty rather than continue to game, if that seems likely to give the partnership its best score. Since the partnership has announced enough combined strength to go for a game contract, it's likely the opponents will be defeated if they compete too high. A doubled penalty may be more than the value of a potential game, or at least be a suitable compensation. On some hands, it might simply be the best result that can be achieved.

Doubles can be challenging in today's game, since there are so many different types: takeout, negative, penalty, responsive, and many more. As a straightforward guideline after the auction has begun with a 2/1 Game Force:

- A double is for penalty if the original overcall is on the doubler's right.
- A double is *cooperative*—high-card showing—if the overcall is on the doubler's left.

This is perhaps clearer if we look at some examples.

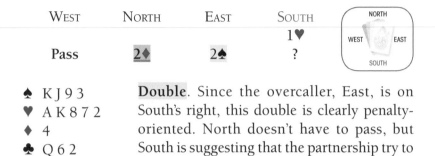

WEST	NORTH	EAST	SOUTH
			1♥
Pass	2♦	2♠	?

♠ K J 9 3
♥ A K 8 7 2
♦ 4
♣ Q 6 2

Double. Since the overcaller, East, is on South's right, this double is clearly penalty-oriented. North doesn't have to pass, but South is suggesting that the partnership try to collect a large penalty instead of continuing to game. South has no fit for responder's suit, and two or three sure trump tricks in the opponent's suit. A great hand to defend with, after partner has shown about 13 or more points.

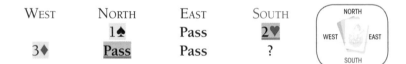

WEST	NORTH	EAST	SOUTH
	1♣	Pass	2♥
3♦	Pass	Pass	?

♠ J 4
♥ A K J 8 3
♦ Q 9 3
♣ Q 7 2

Double. South's 2♥ response created a game force, so North's pass over the 3♦ overcall is still forcing. South doesn't have any clear-cut action. Since the overcaller, West, is on South's left, a double at this point is cooperative. It says: "Partner, you can leave it in for penalty or take it out if you think we can get a better result by bidding."

Since South is sitting to the right of the overcaller, North won't expect South to have a lot of diamond tricks. South's ♦Q, for example, could easily be trapped if West can lead diamonds from dummy. South is simply saying, "I think we have enough combined strength in high cards to defeat their contract, and I don't see a better alternative at this point." So North should not leave the double in for penalty with a very distributional hand, or a fit for South's hearts. But North can pass with a relatively balanced hand.

Summary

OPENER'S REBID AFTER A 2/1 RESPONSE

Opener focuses on describing the shape of the hand. Extra strength can be shown later. Opener's priorities are to:

- Support responder's suit.
- Bid a second suit (except with a minimum when the suit would have to be bid at the three level).
- Rebid a six-card or longer suit.
- Bid notrump (don't worry about stoppers).

RESPONDER'S REBID AFTER A 2/1 RESPONSE

Responder also focuses on deciding WHERE the partnership belongs. Responder's options are to:

- Agree on a trump suit if that hasn't happened already.
- Rebid a six-card or longer suit.
- Suggest notrump if there is no major suit fit.
- Bid fourth suit to get more information from opener.

FOURTH SUIT AFTER 2/1

Responder's* bid of the fourth suit after an initial 2/1 Game Forcing response says either:

- Responder doesn't know what else to bid, or
- Responder has a legitimate two-suited hand
- Responder's next bid will clarify the situation.

    * Opener can also use fourth suit if it is still available.

If the opponents interfere after the 2/1 response, the auction is still forcing to game, unless the partnership decides to double for penalty. A double is for penalty if the original overcall is on the doubler's right; it is cooperative if the overcall is on the doubler's left.

Quiz – Part I

South opens 1♠, and North responds 2♥. What does South rebid with each of the following hands?

WEST	NORTH	EAST	SOUTH
			1♠
Pass	2♥	Pass	?

a) ♠ A K 10 8 5
   ♥ K 9 4
   ♦ K 3
   ♣ 9 8 6

b) ♠ J 10 8 7 6 3
   ♥ 9 4
   ♦ A K 5
   ♣ A 5

c) ♠ K J 8 7 4
   ♥ 6
   ♦ A Q 8 6 2
   ♣ K 4

d) ♠ Q 10 9 7 5
   ♥ Q 5
   ♦ K Q 4
   ♣ A 8 5

e) ♠ A J 9 6 3
   ♥ K J 6
   ♦ A K
   ♣ J 7 2

f) ♠ K Q 9 6 2
   ♥ A 4
   ♦ Q J 5
   ♣ 8 6 3

South opens 1♥ and North responds 2♦. What rebid would South make with each of the following hands?

WEST	NORTH	EAST	SOUTH
			1♥
Pass	2♦	Pass	?

g) ♠ K Q 7 5
   ♥ A J 10 8 3
   ♦ Q 3
   ♣ 7 6

h) ♠ 9 3
   ♥ A Q 10 9 3
   ♦ K 4
   ♣ A Q 9 5

i) ♠ K 3
   ♥ A K J 8 5
   ♦ Q 7 6 2
   ♣ 7 2

j) ♠ A Q
   ♥ K J 8 7 2
   ♦ 6 4
   ♣ Q 9 7 3

k) ♠ 6 3
   ♥ A J 9 8 2
   ♦ K Q 3
   ♣ K 8 2

l) ♠ A J 7
   ♥ K Q 8 5 3
   ♦ 8 4 3
   ♣ K 6

Answers to Quiz – Part I

a) **3♥**. Responder's 2♥ bid promised at least five hearts. Opener's priority is to raise responder's major when there is an eight-card or longer fit.

b) **2♠**. Opener should rebid the spades to show a six-card suit. It's not the strength of the suit that is important, it's the length.

c) **3♦**. Opener should always show a second five-card suit, even it means going to the three level with a minimum hand.

d) **2NT**. A rebid of 2NT describes a balanced hand and doesn't promise any extra strength.

e) **3♥**. Even though opener has a strong hand in support of hearts, there's no need to jump. The raise to 3♥ is forcing. The first step is to agree on the trump suit. Opener can show the extra strength later by moving toward slam.

f) **2NT**. Opener's 2NT rebid only shows a balanced hand. It doesn't promise stoppers in all the unbid suits.

g) **2♠**. Although opener's bid of a higher-ranking suit at the two—level—reverse shows extra values in standard methods, it doesn't promise anything extra playing 2/1 Game Force. Opener's priority is to describe the shape of the hand.

h) **3♣**. Opener can show a four-card suit at the three level with extra values. Here opener has 15 high-card points plus 1 length point for the five-card heart suit.

i) **3♦**. Opener shows support for responder's minor by raising to the three level.

j) **2NT**. With a minimum opening bid and only a weak four-card club suit, opener doesn't have enough to bid the suit at the three level. A 2NT rebid is a reasonable description of the hand.

k) **3♦**. Opener can raise responder's minor with good three-card support.

l) **2NT**. With poor three-card support for opener's minor suit, 2NT is a more descriptive rebid than raising responder's minor.

Quiz – Part II

North opens 1♥, South responds 2♣, and opener rebids 2♦. What does South rebid with each of the following hands?

West	North	East	South
	1♥	Pass	2♣
Pass	2♦	Pass	?

a) ♠ 7 2
   ♥ Q 9 4
   ♦ K Q J
   ♣ A Q 8 4 3

b) ♠ 8 6 2
   ♥ 5
   ♦ A J 8 3
   ♣ A K J 9 5

c) ♠ 9 7
   ♥ A 2
   ♦ K 6 2
   ♣ A J 10 9 7 3

d) ♠ K 10 3
   ♥ Q 4
   ♦ J 10 7
   ♣ A Q J 8 3

e) ♠ A K J
   ♥ 10 4
   ♦ K 9 3
   ♣ K Q J 5 2

f) ♠ 6 5 2
   ♥ K 4
   ♦ A K 8
   ♣ K 9 8 5 2

North opens 1♠, South responds 2♦, and opener rebids 2♥. What rebid would South make with each of the following hands?

West	North	East	South
	1♠	Pass	2♦
Pass	2♥	Pass	?

g) ♠ Q 4
   ♥ 10 8 6 3
   ♦ A K 8 3
   ♣ A J 8

h) ♠ A Q 5
   ♥ A 2
   ♦ K Q 9 8 5 2
   ♣ 8 4

i) ♠ 4
   ♥ 9 3
   ♦ A K J 7 3
   ♣ A K Q 8 2

j) ♠ 6
   ♥ Q J 4
   ♦ A Q 8 5 2
   ♣ K J 10 3

k) ♠ 8 3
   ♥ K 7
   ♦ A K J 9 7 5 2
   ♣ Q 3

l) ♠ Q 4
   ♥ A 9 3
   ♦ A Q J 8 5
   ♣ 7 6 2

Answers to Quiz – Part II

a) **2♥**. Time to agree on the trumps. Although the diamonds are stronger, opener has only promised a four-card suit and is known to hold five hearts. Agreeing on hearts is responder's top priority.

b) **3♦**. Here responder has support for opener's second suit and can show that by raising. No need to jump; 3♦ is forcing.

c) **3♣**. There may be only a seven-card fit in hearts or in diamonds. To continue the search for a suitable fit, responder can rebid the club suit, waiting to hear what opener says next.

d) **2NT**. With a stopper in spades and a balanced hand, responder can suggest playing in notrump.

e) **2NT**. Although responder usually has a minimum balanced hand to rebid 2NT, responder can also hold 18 or more points. The first step is to suggest notrump. Responder can show the extra strength later.

f) **2♠**. Responder doesn't have enough hearts or diamonds to support either suit, and can't rebid the weak five-card club suit. Responder doesn't want to bid 2NT with no stopper in spades. So responder bids the fourth suit, passing the next decision back to opener.

g) **3♥**. Responder shows support for opener's second suit by raising to the three level.

h) **2♠**. With three-card support for spades, responder wants to agree on trumps. That takes priority over rebidding diamonds.

i) **3♣**. With a two-suiter in diamonds and clubs, responder shows the second suit. Since 3♣ is fourth suit, opener won't know responder really has clubs until responder bids them again on the next round.

j) **2NT**. With no known eight-card major-suit fit, responder can suggest playing in notrump. There's little point in bidding clubs, since that is the fourth suit. Opener will assume it is a probe for notrump, probably with no club stopper.

k) **3♦**. Responder can show the long diamond suit by rebidding it. The partnership could belong in 3NT or 5♦, or perhaps one of opener's suits. It's too soon to know.

l) **3♣**. With no clear-cut action, responder bids the fourth suit, 3♣. Opener will usually bid 3NT with a club stopper. If not, opener will find some other bid, and the partnership may avoid playing in 3NT.

Quiz – Part III

What call does South make with the given hand in each of the following auctions?

	WEST	NORTH	EAST	SOUTH	
a)	WEST	NORTH	EAST	SOUTH (Opener)	♠ A J 9 8 7 3
				1♠	♥ 9 8 6 3
					♦ A Q
	Pass	2♣	Pass	?	♣ 4
b)	WEST	NORTH	EAST	SOUTH (Opener)	♠ A J 8 7 6 3
			Pass	1♠	♥ 8 3
					♦ A K 7 5
	Pass	2♣	Pass	?	♣ 4
c)	WEST	NORTH	EAST	SOUTH (Opener)	♠ 10 8 4
				1♥	♥ A J 9 8 3
					♦ A 4
	Pass	2♦	2♠	?	♣ Q J 3
d)	WEST	NORTH	EAST	SOUTH (Opener)	♠ A K 8 6 3
			Pass	1♠	♥ A 3
					♦ 6 4
	Pass	2♦	3♣	?	♣ Q J 9 6
e)	WEST	NORTH	EAST	SOUTH (Opener)	♠ 7 3
				1♥	♥ K Q 8 7 3
					♦ A K J 2
	Pass	2♣	Pass	2♦	♣ 4 2
	Pass	3♣	Pass	?	
f)	WEST	NORTH	EAST	SOUTH (Responder)	♠ J 7 5
					♥ J 3
		1♥	Pass	2♦	♦ A K J 8 5
	2♠	Pass	Pass	?	♣ K 10 8

Answers to Quiz – Part III

a) **2♥**. Even with a good six-card spade suit, opener should not bypass a four-card heart suit on the rebid. Partner could easily have a four-card heart suit, but could not respond 2♥ since that would promise five.

b) **2♦**. With 6-4 distribution, opener usually shows the four-card suit on the rebid if it can conveniently be bid at the two level. The 1♠ opening has promised five or more spades, and the 2♦ bid shows four or more diamonds. So responder will know at least nine of opener's cards. If opener rebids 2♠, responder will only know that opener has a sixth spade. This is the '6-4-6' approach.

c) **Pass**. If East had not interfered, South would have to bid something. When East overcalls, however, South can pass with nothing particular to say. South doesn't want to bid 2NT without a spade stopper. South's pass is forcing, since game has not yet been reached.

d) **Double**. Although the partnership is generally headed for at least game, it doesn't need to pass up an opportunity to collect a large penalty if the opponents come into the auction. With a relatively balanced hand and no good fit with partner's suit, South's double suggests defending for penalty.

e) **3♠**. Opener has already shown five hearts and four diamonds. Over responder's 3♣ rebid, opener doesn't want to bid 3♥, which would tend to show a sixth heart, or bid 3♦, which would show a fifth diamond. Opener doesn't want to bypass 3NT by raising to 4♣, but opener doesn't want to bid notrump with nothing in spades. So opener is left with bidding the fourth suit, 3♠, saying, "I don't know what else to do at this point!" Hopefully, responder will be able to take it from there. Perhaps responder can bid 3NT with a spade stopper.

f) **Double**. Opener's pass is forcing, since the 2♦ response committed the partnership to game. With a doubleton heart, a five-card diamond suit, and no spade stopper, South has no good descriptive bid at this point. The best choice is to double, leaving the next decision to partner. This is not a pure penalty double since the overcaller, West, is sitting over any spade holding South might have. It is a cooperative double, saying that the partnership likely has enough in combined high-card strength to defeat 2♠, but that opener can bid again with a distributional hand and nothing much in spades.

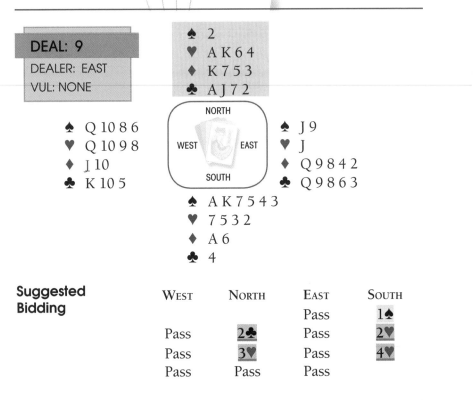

DEAL: 9
DEALER: EAST
VUL: NONE

♠ 2
♥ A K 6 4
♦ K 7 5 3
♣ A J 7 2

♠ Q 10 8 6
♥ Q 10 9 8
♦ J 10
♣ K 10 5

WEST   EAST

NORTH

SOUTH

♠ J 9
♥ J
♦ Q 9 8 4 2
♣ Q 9 8 6 3

♠ A K 7 5 4 3
♥ 7 5 3 2
♦ A 6
♣ 4

Suggested Bidding

WEST	NORTH	EAST	SOUTH
		Pass	1♠
Pass	2♣	Pass	2♥
Pass	3♥	Pass	4♥
Pass	Pass	Pass	

East passes. South opens 1♠, and North bids 2♣, following the standard style of responding with four-card suits 'up the line'—cheapest first. North can't respond 2♥ because that would promise a five-card suit.

Although South has a good six-card spade suit, opener shouldn't bypass the opportunity to show a four-card heart suit, even a poor one. The partnership is looking to find an eight-card major-suit fit, and that won't happen if neither player can bid a four-card suit.

After opener shows the four-card heart suit, responder raises to agree on the trump suit. There's no need to jump; the 3♥ rebid is forcing. With a minimum opening bid and a poor heart suit, South settles for game, and North doesn't have enough to venture any further.

Suggested Opening Lead

West will probably lead the ♦J, top of the touching cards in the unbid suit.

Suggested Play

Deals like this can be complex if declarer starts counting losers rather than focusing on winners. Declarer has four spade losers and at least one heart loser more if the hearts break unfavorably, as on the actual deal. Declarer could plan on drawing two rounds of trumps and then establishing the spade suit by trumping one or two spades in dummy. Declarer can make the contract this way, despite the bad heart break.

However, it is probably more straightforward to count winners. Declarer has seven tricks on top: ♠A-K, ♥A-K, ♦A-K, and ♣A. Three more are needed. These can be developed by trumping two clubs in the South hand and trumping one or more spades in the dummy. In fact, declarer can make eleven tricks this way on the actual lie of the cards. Declarer wins the first diamond and plays the ♥A-K. When East shows out. Declarer plays the ♣A and ruffs a club. Then the ♠A-K and a spade ruff. Another club ruff, a spade ruff, and the remaining high diamond, and declarer has eleven winners. West's two remaining hearts take the last two tricks.

Suggested Defense

There's nothing the defenders can do if declarer takes the winners and *crossruffs* for ten or eleven tricks. However, if declarer plays a third round of trumps after taking the ♥A-K, West can win and draw declarer's remaining trumps, holding declarer to seven tricks.

Also, if declarer plays the ♥A-K and tries to ruff one of dummy's diamonds, West can overruff and draw another round of trumps to defeat the contract. Declarer should ruff clubs rather than diamonds. With six diamonds and only five clubs between the North-South hands, it is less likely that West is short in clubs rather than diamonds.

Conclusion

With best defense, North-South can only make seven tricks in a notrump contract and nine tricks in a spade contract. The 4-4 heart fit will produce ten or eleven tricks. South should not focus on the quality of the heart suit when choosing a rebid, only on the number of hearts.

Finding the heart suit on this deal is important for North-South. South has to choose to rebid 2♥, even with a weak four-card heart suit and a six-card spade suit.

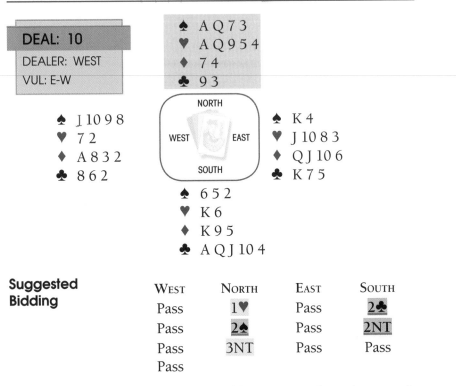

DEAL: 10
DEALER: WEST
VUL: E-W

♠ A Q 7 3
♥ A Q 9 5 4
♦ 7 4
♣ 9 3

NORTH

♠ J 10 9 8
♥ 7 2
♦ A 8 3 2
♣ 8 6 2

WEST   EAST

♠ K 4
♥ J 10 8 3
♦ Q J 10 6
♣ K 7 5

SOUTH

♠ 6 5 2
♥ K 6
♦ K 9 5
♣ A Q J 10 4

**Suggested
Bidding**

WEST	NORTH	EAST	SOUTH
Pass	1♥	Pass	2♣
Pass	2♠	Pass	2NT
Pass	3NT	Pass	Pass
Pass			

West passes. North opens the five-card heart suit, and South responds
2♣. North can make the natural rebid of 2♠ to show the second suit.
Although this is technically a reverse, most partnerships using 2/1 do
not play that a two-level reverse necessarily promises extra values after
a 2/1 response. After all, the partnership is already committed to at least
game. The focus is on WHERE. Any extra values can be shown later.

After North shows the spade suit, South has an easy notrump bid.
South only needs to bid 2NT, since this is still forcing. It gives North
an opportunity to show extra values or distribution. North could have
a 'real' reverse, with 17 or more points. On the actual deal, North has
nothing extra to show and simply raises to game. The partnership stops
in the best contract.

Suggested Opening Lead

West might chose to lead the ♦2. However, West knows South likely has
some strength in diamonds for the notrump bid, so West might try leading
through the strength in dummy with the ♠J, top of the solid sequence.

Suggested Play

On a diamond lead, declarer will win a trick with the ♦K, and then has little choice but to try the club finesse.

On a spade lead, declarer must be careful. It's tempting to take the spade finesse by playing dummy's ♠Q, but if the finesses loses, the defenders might switch to a diamond, defeating the contract when the ♦A is unfavorably located—as in the actual deal. Declarer doesn't need the spade finesse if the club finesse is working and either the hearts or clubs divide favorably. So declarer should win the ♠A and lead the ♣9, taking the club finesse when East follows with a low card. Declarer can repeat the club finesse, and when the suit divides 3-3, declarer has five club tricks to go with the ♠A and three heart tricks.

Suggested Defense

As it turns out, the best lead is a spade. If declarer tries the finesse, East can win the ♠K and switch to the ♦Q. This traps declarer's ♦K, and the defenders get four diamond tricks to go with the ♠K and defeat 3NT.

Conclusion

In standard bidding, the auction might go awkwardly:

WEST	NORTH	EAST	SOUTH
Pass	1♥	Pass	2♣
Pass	2♥?	Pass	4♥?
Pass	Pass	Pass	

North has a dilemma after the 2♣ response. In standard methods, a 2♠ rebid would be a reverse, showing extra values and committing the partnership to game. With a minimum hand, North doesn't want to force the partnership to game when there might be no suitable trump fit and responder could have as few as 10 or 11 points. North might choose to rebid the five-card heart suit rather than bid 2NT with no diamond stopper.

A 2♥ rebid by North would give South a problem. South wants to be in game, but doesn't want to jump to 3NT with nothing in spades. South might choose to put the partnership in game in hearts, on the assumption that North likely has a six-card heart suit. 4♥ is likely to be defeated. The defenders can take two diamonds, a heart, and a spade.

Using 2/1, the partnership has a relaxed time describing the hands and searching for the best contract.

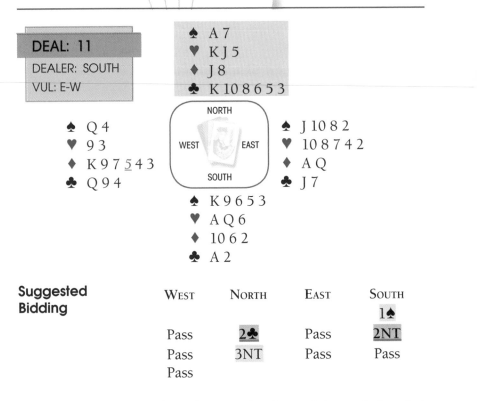

DEAL: 11

DEALER: SOUTH

VUL: E-W

NORTH

♠ A 7
♥ K J 5
♦ J 8
♣ K 10 8 6 5 3

WEST

♠ Q 4
♥ 9 3
♦ K 9 7 5 4 3
♣ Q 9 4

EAST

♠ J 10 8 2
♥ 10 8 7 4 2
♦ A Q
♣ J 7

SOUTH

♠ K 9 6 5 3
♥ A Q 6
♦ 10 6 2
♣ A 2

Suggested Bidding

WEST	NORTH	EAST	SOUTH
			1♠
Pass	2♣	Pass	2NT
Pass	3NT	Pass	Pass
Pass			

After South opens 1♠ and North responds 2♣, South has to find a rebid to describe the hand. With a balanced hand, South rebids 2NT. The 2NT rebid doesn't promise stoppers in both the unbid suits, so South doesn't need to be concerned about holding three low diamonds. The focus is on describing the shape.

Although North could rebid 3♣ to show the sixth club, with a relatively balanced hand, North judges to raise to 3NT. It should be easier to take nine tricks than eleven.

The partnership reaches 3NT with no diamond stopper. That's okay. The defenders might not lead a diamond; or the missing diamonds might be divided 4-4; or the defenders' diamonds may be blocked, preventing them from taking all their diamond tricks right away.

Suggested Opening Lead

West will lead the ♦5, fourth from longest and strongest.

Suggested Play

Declarer will be a little concerned when dummy comes down, because the defenders have led diamonds, and threaten to take five or more tricks before South even gains the lead. However, a fortunate lie in diamonds prevents the opponents from running the suit. After East wins the ♦A-Q, East has to switch to another suit, and declarer gains the lead.

Declarer's challenge is not over. There are only seven winners: the ♠A-K, ♥A-K-Q, and ♣A-K. Two more tricks are needed, and declarer must avoid giving West the lead. West is the *dangerous opponent*, ready to take the setting tricks in diamonds on gaining the lead.

Declarer could hope to develop two extra winners from the spade suit, if the missing spades are divided 3-3 and West can be kept off lead when a trick has to be lost. A 3-3 break is against the odds, and it may be difficult to keep West from gaining the lead. The club suit presents a much better opportunity. Declarer only needs the missing clubs to be divided 3-2 – which is with the odds – and it will be possible to keep West from gaining the lead unless West holds three clubs including the ♣Q and ♣J.

Declarer plays the ♣A and leads a low club toward dummy. When West follows with the ♣9, declarer plays dummy's ♣10, losing the trick that must be lost to East, the safe opponent. Dummy's remaining clubs are winners and West never gains the lead. Declarer makes an overtrick.

If West had produced the ♣Q or ♣J on the second trick, declarer would win dummy's ♣K and play a third round of clubs, hoping East held the remaining high club. Not a sure thing, but the best chance.

Suggested Defense

West can't afford to overtake East's ♦Q with the ♦K on the second round of diamonds, because that would establish South's ♦10 as a winner. Unfortunately for the defenders, the diamond suit is blocked. West will have to hope to gain the lead in spades or clubs to be able to take the rest of the diamond winners.

Conclusion

Whenever the partnership has a minor-suit fit, playing game in 3NT rather than 5♣ or 5♦ is always a consideration. On this deal, 3NT cannot be defeated, whereas 4♠ or 5♣ cannot make against good defense. Even without a stopper in one of the other suits, it may still be easier to take nine tricks in notrump than eleven tricks in a suit.

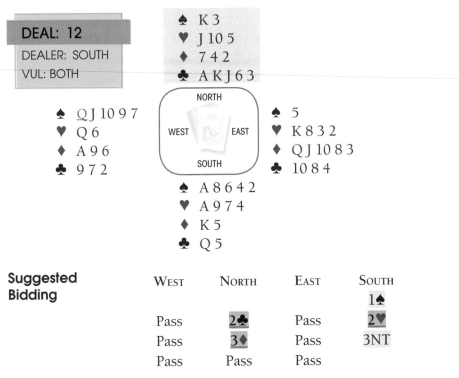

DEAL: 12

DEALER: SOUTH

VUL: BOTH

NORTH
♠ K 3
♥ J 10 5
♦ 7 4 2
♣ A K J 6 3

WEST
♠ Q J 10 9 7
♥ Q 6
♦ A 9 6
♣ 9 7 2

EAST
♠ 5
♥ K 8 3 2
♦ Q J 10 8 3
♣ 10 8 4

SOUTH
♠ A 8 6 4 2
♥ A 9 7 4
♦ K 5
♣ Q 5

Suggested Bidding

WEST	NORTH	EAST	SOUTH
			1♠
Pass	2♣	Pass	2♥
Pass	3♦	Pass	3NT
Pass	Pass	Pass	

South opens 1♠ and rebids 2♥ over North's 2♣ response. North now has to find a rebid. North doesn't want to agree on spades as the trump suit with only a doubleton, and doesn't want to raise hearts with only three-card support. A rebid of 3♣ would tend to show a six-card suit, and North doesn't want to bid 3NT with no stopper in the only unbid suit—the one the opponents are most likely to lead. So North bids the fourth suit, 3♦. This says nothing about diamonds. It is simply forcing, hoping opener's next bid will help get the partnership to the best contract.

Since North could have bid 2NT with a stopper in diamonds, South is aware that North doesn't necessarily have anything in diamonds. However, South is holding a stopper in that suit, and can bid 3NT. The partnership reaches 3NT from the 'correct' side.

Suggested Opening Lead

There is no unbid suit, although West should be aware that North's 3♦ bid did not necessarily promise anything in diamonds. West might lead a diamond, but with such solid spades, is more likely to lead the ♠Q.

Suggested Play

If West leads a diamond, declarer will get a trick with the ♦K and have nine tricks: two spades, a heart, a diamond, and five clubs. If West leads a spade, declarer will need to establish a ninth trick.

One possibility is the diamond finesse. Declarer could lead a diamond from dummy, hoping East has the ♦A, a 50% chance. Another possibility is spades. If the missing spades are divided 3-3 or 4-2, declarer can develop an extra trick in that suit through length. However, West's opening lead makes it unlikely that spades are dividing favorably.[28] By far the best possibility, however, is the heart suit. Declarer has a 75% chance of developing at least one extra trick in hearts.

Declarer can win dummy's ♠K and lead the ♥J. If East covers with the ♥K, declarer can win the ♥A and drive out West's ♥Q. If, as is more likely, East doesn't play the ♥K when the ♥J is led, declarer plays low and West wins this trick with the ♥Q. After regaining the lead, declarer can later lead the ♥10 from dummy, trapping East's ♥K.

Playing hearts this way will give declarer an extra trick if East has the ♥K, or the ♥Q, or both the ♥K and ♥Q. It only fails if West holds both the ♥K and ♥Q.[29] It is also the safest way to make the contract. Declarer doesn't mind losing a heart trick to West, since West is the safe opponent. West can't lead diamonds without giving declarer a trick with the ♦K. East is the dangerous opponent. If East gains the lead and leads a diamond, South's ♦K may be trapped if West has the ♦A—as on the actual deal—and the defenders may take enough tricks to defeat 3NT.

Suggested Defense

If North becomes declarer in 3NT, East defeats the contract by leading a diamond. The defenders get the first five tricks. If South is declarer, 3NT can't be defeated unless declarer lets East gain the lead.

Conclusion

Playing 2/1 Game Force, a bid of the fourth suit by either responder or opener is rarely suggesting that suit as trumps. It is usually a probe, asking for further help from partner in deciding **WHERE** to play the contract.

---

[28] Declarer could let West's ♠Q win the first trick, taking a loss early in that suit. On the actual deal, however, this doesn't help when the suit divides 5-1.

[29] If East held both the ♥K and ♥Q, East could not be prevented from gaining the lead. Declarer would then have to hope East also held the ♦A.

One key to effective slam bidding is to know when to use Blackwood and what to do when it is not appropriate. As Easley Blackwood was the first to admit, Blackwood is not the answer to all slam decisions. The sole function of Blackwood is to discover partner's number of aces. On many hands, though, quantity is not the answer; what we seek is location, location, location.

— Marty Bergen
More Points Schmoints! (1999)

The Choice Between Game and Slam

The initial 2/1 response commits the partnership to at least game, and allows both opener and responder the opportunity to explore WHERE the partnership belongs in a relaxed manner, without having to worry about showing both distribution and strength at the same time. Once the partnership has agreed on a trump suit, or notrump, the focus can now shift to the remaining question, HOW HIGH: Game or Slam?

Focus on How High

Game is assured, but does the partnership have enough combined strength for slam? The basic guideline is that the partnership needs about 33 points to consider a small slam and about 37 points to think about a grand slam. The factors to bear in mind are:

- Combining both high-card points and distributional points.
- Fit.
- Controls.

HIGH-CARD POINTS

Slams in notrump are typically bid in a quantitative manner, on combined high-card strength alone. After one partner has shown a balanced or semi-balanced hand within a narrow point-count range, the other partner can add up the combined strength and decide whether there is enough to bid a slam.

OPENER	RESPONDER
♠ K Q 3	♠ A 7 6
♥ K 9 5	♥ A Q 7
♦ K Q J 4	♦ A 6 2
♣ 8 6 3	♣ K Q J 5

OPENER	RESPONDER
1♦	2♣
2NT	6NT
PASS	

The opening 1♦ bid shows about 13 or more points. Holding 20 high-card points, responder knows the partnership has enough combined strength to go for a small slam, but doesn't yet know WHERE. When opener rebids 2NT, showing a balanced hand, responder can simply take the partnership right to 6NT. This is a straight quantitative auction.

Responder's 6NT bid would be a signoff in standard methods, since opener's 2NT rebid is limited to about 12-14 points. Opener would have to jump to 3NT with a stronger hand, since the 2NT rebid would not be forcing. Playing 2/1 Game Force, however, opener's 2NT rebid could be a minimum hand, but could also be a much stronger hand of about 18–19 points. Opener doesn't have to jump because the 2NT rebid is forcing. So opener might bid again in this situation:

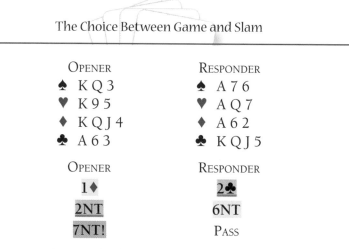

OPENER	RESPONDER
♠ K Q 3	♠ A 7 6
♥ K 9 5	♥ A Q 7
♦ K Q J 4	♦ A 6 2
♣ A 6 3	♣ K Q J 5

OPENER	RESPONDER
1♦	2♣
2NT	6NT
7NT!	PASS

Here opener has 18 high-card points, too much to open 1NT. After responder raises to 6NT based on the assumption that opener has only a minimum balanced hand of about 12–14 points, opener can raise to 7NT with extra values. Opener has 4 or 5 more points than responder is expecting, so the partnership should have at least 37 combined points, enough for a grand slam.

Although combined strength for notrump is mainly based on high-card points, long suits can also be valuable. Most players add 1 length point for a five-card suit, 2 for a six-card suit, and so on.

OPENER	RESPONDER
♠ K J 8 7 3	♠ A Q
♥ K 8 2	♥ A 7 3
♦ Q 4	♦ A K J 8 3
♣ K 6 3	♣ J 9 5

OPENER	RESPONDER
1♠	2♦
2NT	6NT
PASS	

Opener has only 12 high-card points, but adds 1 length point for the fifth spade suit and opens 1♠. Responder has only 19 high-card points, but adds 1 length point for the fifth diamond. So the partnership reaches 6NT with only 31 combined high-card points. However, the five-card suits prove very useful. On normal breaks, declarer has twelve tricks off the top: five spades, two hearts, and five diamonds.

If it is unclear whether the partnership has enough combined strength for slam in notrump, either partner can make a quantitative—invitational—raise.

OPENER	RESPONDER
♠ A J 5	♠ K Q 6
♥ Q 10 7 3 2	♥ J 4
♦ K 10 3	♦ A 9 8
♣ Q 4	♣ A K J 7 5

OPENER	RESPONDER
1♥	2♣
2NT	4NT
PASS	

Responder's 4NT bid is not Blackwood, since no trump suit has been agreed upon. It is an invitation to slam—in the same way that a raise of an opening 1NT to 2NT would be an invitation to game. With a minimum opening bid, opener rejects the invitation by passing.

OPENER	RESPONDER
♠ A Q J 8 3	♠ 10 4
♥ A J 5	♥ K 8 2
♦ K 6	♦ A Q J 10 4
♣ K 8 2	♣ A 10 5

OPENER	RESPONDER
1♠	2♦
2NT	3NT
4NT	6NT
PASS	

Opener has 18 high-card points plus 1 length point for the five-card suit, a hand too strong to open 1NT. After the game-forcing 2♦ response, opener doesn't need to jump to show the extra strength; the 2NT rebid is forcing. When responder shows a willingness to play in notrump, opener now shows the extra strength with an invitational raise to 4NT.

With a minimum balanced hand, opener would simply pass the raise to 3NT. Holding 14 high-card points plus 1 length point for the five-card suit, responder has enough to accept. Responder knows opener must have a balanced hand of about 18–19 points, so the partnership has enough to go for the slam bonus.

Quantitative bidding is based on sheer power. Just as a raise of 1NT to 3NT doesn't guarantee that the partnership can make nine tricks—the opponents might take the first five tricks, or all the finesses might lose—there is no assurance that there will be enough tricks in a slam reached in the same manner. The suits might break badly, or the opponents might have the ace and king in the same suit and take them right off the top. Still, it's usually the best way to bid slams when both hands are reasonably balanced. The opponents don't always find the best lead!

DISTRIBUTIONAL POINTS

Long suits are typically valuable whether the partnership plays in a notrump or suit contract. They provide a potential source of tricks. So both opener and responder generally count length points in addition to high-card points when valuing the hand.

Short suits may or may not be of value. In notrump contracts, they can be a liability. In suit contracts, they can be very valuable in a side suit after a trump fit has been found. They can prevent the opponents from taking winners in a suit, and may provide an additional source of tricks for declarer through ruffing. However, shortness won't be of much value if it is partner's suggested trump suit or opposite a lot of high-card strength in partner's hand. So the guideline is to value points for shortness—*dummy points*[30]—only after a trump fit has been found.

---

[30] Points for shortness are typically referred to as dummy points, since they will usually be in the hand that is going to be put down on the table as the dummy.

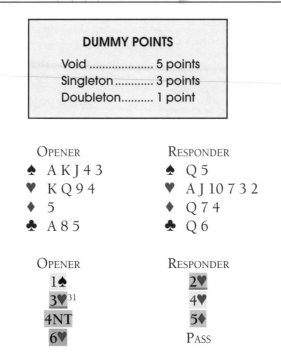

DUMMY POINTS

Void .... 5 points
Singleton .... 3 points
Doubleton .... 1 point

OPENER	RESPONDER
♠ A K J 4 3	♠ Q 5
♥ K Q 9 4	♥ A J 10 7 3 2
♦ 5	♦ Q 7 4
♣ A 8 5	♣ Q 6

OPENER	RESPONDER
1♠	2♥
3♥[31]	4♥
4NT	5♦
6♥	PASS

Opener has 17 high-card points and can add 3 dummy points for the singleton diamond once the heart fit is uncovered. That's enough to check for aces, even though responder shows nothing extra. There are only 28 combined high-card points, but the added points for distribution—responder for length and opener for shortness—make slam a good proposition.

---

[31] Opener could make a splinter bid of 4♦ if the partnership uses that convention.

FIT

One advantage of 2/1 is that it provides a way for the partnership to leisurely explore for a suitable trump fit. Finding a fit is crucial, especially when it comes to slam bidding. For example, consider these combined hands:

OPENER	RESPONDER
♠ A Q J 7 5 3	♠ 4
♥ A K Q J	♥ 9 8 3
♦ 5 4	♦ K Q J
♣ 3	♣ A Q J 6 4 2

OPENER	RESPONDER
1♠	2♣
2♥	3♣
3♠	3NT
PASS	

Opener has 17 high-card points plus 2 length points for the six-card suit. Responder has 13 high-card points plus 2 length points for the six-card suit. That's a total of 34 combined points, more than enough for slam. But with no suitable trump fit, the partnership settles for game. It will be challenging to find a good source of tricks, and entries back and forth between the two hands will be difficult or non-existent. Now consider these hands:

OPENER	RESPONDER
♠ A J 8 6 3	♠ 4
♥ A 7 4	♥ K Q 10 8 6 3 2
♦ K 9 3	♦ A 4
♣ 7 3	♣ K Q 4

OPENER	RESPONDER
1♠	2♥
3♥	4NT
5♥	6♥
PASS	

When the partnership finds a fit, all the distributional factors come into play. Here there are only 26 combined points, but once opener supports hearts, responder can imagine that there will likely be twelve tricks if opener has two aces.

CONTROLS

Once the partnership has found a suitable trump fit and knows there is likely enough combined strength to consider a slam, one final consideration is *controls*. A control is a holding that prevents the opponents from taking too many tricks in a suit. An ace is a *first-round control*, since it stops the opponents from taking the first trick in a suit. In a trump contract, a void can also serve as a first-round control, since it prevents the opponents from taking the first trick in a suit. A king represents a *second-round control*. The opponents can take the first trick with the ace, but the king will stop them on the second round[32]. In a trump contract, a singleton can serve the same role as a king—a second-round control.

CONTROLS IN A SUIT CONTRACT	
First-round control	Ace or void
Second-round control	King or singleton

For a small slam, the partnership needs first-round control in three suits, and at least second-round control in the fourth. Otherwise, the opponents can take the first two tricks before declarer gets started. To bid a grand slam, the partnership needs first-round control in all four suits. It's discomforting to watch the opponents take the first trick when we have contracted to take all thirteen!

How does the partnership discover whether it holds enough controls to bid a slam? There are two principle methods:

- Blackwood
- Control-showing bids

CONTROL REQUIREMENTS	
Small Slam	First-round control in three suits; at least second-round control in the fourth
Grand Slam	First-round control in every suit.

[32] If the king is in the dummy, declarer may need the opponents' ace favorably located, but at least the contract will have a chance.

The Blackwood Convention[33]

Blackwood is the most popular way to find out about the aces and kings held by the partnership, but it is often overused.

WHEN TO USE BLACKWOOD

The player bidding Blackwood assumes captaincy of the partnership. Based on partner's responses, the captain will decide whether to bid a slam. To use Blackwood, the captain should be fairly certain:

- A trump suit has been agreed.
- There is likely to be enough combined strength for a slam.
- All that needs to be known is the number of aces and/or kings held by the partnership.

OPENER	RESPONDER
♠ A Q J 7 6	♠ K 4
♥ J 9 5 2	♥ K Q 10 8 7 4 3
♦ K Q J	♦ 5
♣ 2	♣ A K Q

OPENER	RESPONDER
1♠	2♥
3♥	4NT
5♦	5♥
PASS	

Once opener raises hearts, the decision on **WHERE** is resolved, and it is only a matter of **HOW HIGH**. With 17 high-card points plus 3 length points, responder knows the partnership has enough combined strength to be in the slam zone. The only consideration is whether the partnership has enough controls. Responder uses Blackwood to ask about aces. When opener shows one ace, responder knows the partnership is missing two aces and signs off in 5♥.

---

[33] Appendix 8 describes the Blackwood convention and Key Card variations.

Opener has a hand worth 17 points—14 high-card points plus 3 dummy points. However, even with extra values, opener should not override responder's decision to stop in 5♥. By using Blackwood, responder assumed captaincy of the partnership. Responder knows how many aces the partnership holds; opener does not. So 5♥ is a signoff, not an invitation.

Although the partnership has more than enough combined strength for a slam, it can't make a slam because the opponents can take the first two tricks, the ♦A and ♥A. Blackwood is a form of insurance to keep the partnership out of bad slams.

Let's change opener's hand a little:

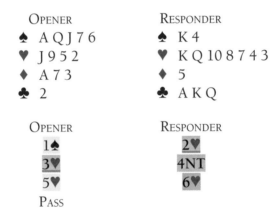

OPENER	RESPONDER
♠ A Q J 7 6	♠ K 4
♥ J 9 5 2	♥ K Q 10 8 7 4 3
♦ A 7 3	♦ 5
♣ 2	♣ A K Q

OPENER	RESPONDER
1♠	2♥
3♥	4NT
5♥	6♥
PASS	

Now opener has 2 fewer high-card points, but they are the 'right' points. When opener shows two aces, responder can confidently bid the small slam.

Let's change opener's hand again:

OPENER	RESPONDER
♠ A 10 8 7 6	♠ K 4
♥ A 9 5 2	♥ K Q 10 8 7 4 3
♦ A 7 3	♦ 5
♣ 2	♣ A K Q

OPENER	RESPONDER
1♠	2♥
3♥	4NT
5♠	7♥
PASS	

The same total high-card points in opener's hand, but responder can bid a grand slam when opener shows three aces. There are 13 top tricks: two spades, seven hearts, one diamond, and three clubs. Responder could actually bid 7NT rather than 7♥!

WHEN TO AVOID BLACKWOOD

Blackwood doesn't handle all situations involving controls. We should avoid automatically using Blackwood with:

1) Two or more cards in an unbid suit with no ace or king.
2) A void.
3) A slam-invitational hand.

1)

	OPENER	RESPONDER
♠	K 10 8 7 5	A Q
♥	A 9 5	K Q J 8 7 6 3
♦	10 5	Q 7
♣	A Q 3	K 4

OPENER	RESPONDER
1♠	2♥
3♥	?

After opener agrees on hearts, responder has enough strength to consider slam, but if responder bids 4NT and opener shows two aces, what does responder do now? The partnership is missing only one ace, but if responder bids 6♥, the defenders will likely take the first two diamonds. However, if one of opener's aces were the ♦A and the other the ♥A or ♣A, 6♥ would be an excellent contract.

The problem in using Blackwood is responder's diamond holding. With no control in the unbid diamond suit, responder has to be cautious. In general, to take over the captaincy and use Blackwood we should be reasonably sure the partnership has at least second-round control in every suit.

That's not easy to do, although we'll look at how we might address this issue shortly. However, we can usually make the assumption that partner holds either first- or second-round control in a suit partner has bid. Not always perfect, but a reasonable approach. It's an unbid suit in which we hold no control that we are most concerned about.

2)

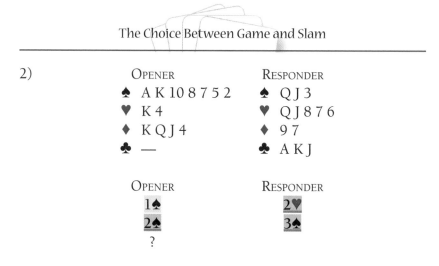

OPENER	RESPONDER
♠ A K 10 8 7 5 2	♠ Q J 3
♥ K 4	♥ Q J 8 7 6
♦ K Q J 4	♦ 9 7
♣ —	♣ A K J

OPENER	RESPONDER
1♠	2♥
2♠	3♠
?	

Opener again has enough that slam is likely once the trump suit is determined, but using Blackwood is not the best approach. Responder's reply to Blackwood would show one ace, and opener would still not know what to do. If responder has the ♦A or ♥A, the partnership belongs in 6♠. If responder has the ♣A, as on the actual deal, the defenders can take the first two tricks with the ♦A and ♥A.

The problem is that opener holds a void in clubs. Opener doesn't need to know about the ♣A. Opener wants to know about specific aces, the ♦A and ♥A. We'll address a way to handle this in a moment, but another approach might be for opener to simply jump to slam and hope for the best. Given no information to help them, the defenders may not take the ♥A quickly enough, and declarer may be able to discard both hearts on the ♣A-K. The point is that jumping to slam holding a void is likely to be at least as effective as bidding Blackwood!

3)

OPENER	RESPONDER
♠ Q 7 6 5 2	♠ A 4
♥ A 4 2	♥ K J 8 7 6 3
♦ 9 3	♦ A 6
♣ A Q J	♣ K 8 5

OPENER	RESPONDER
1♠	2♥
3♥	?

If responder bids 4NT, opener will show two aces. The partnership holds all the aces, but that doesn't make 6♥ a good slam. Declarer will likely have to lose a spade trick and a diamond trick, and might also lose a trick to the ♥Q.

The problem here is that responder isn't strong enough to assume captaincy and commit the partnership to slam based on the response to Blackwood. Instead, responder wants to show interest in slam and get opener involved in the decision.

So how does the partnership deal with such situations? Let's take a look.

Control-Showing Bids

Blackwood reveals only how many aces and kings partner holds. If we need to know which aces and kings partner holds, we must turn to control-showing bids. Control-showing also helps to deal with voids as first-round controls and singletons as second-round controls.

Showing controls takes a different approach to slam bidding than Blackwood. Instead of asking partner about the number of aces held, we show an ace, or some other control, that we hold. In turn, partner is expected to show a control, and the bidding continues back and forth until the partnership discovers whether there are enough controls to bid to a slam.

RECOGNIZING A CONTROL BID

How do we know when we're into a control-showing situation in a 2/1 auction? Once the partnership has agreed on Where, the only remaining question is How High: Game or Slam? If we aren't interested in slam, we simply stop in game in the agreed trump suit. So:

SHOWING CONTROLS AFTER 2/1

Once the trump suit has been agreed, the bid of another suit is a control-showing bid with interest in slam.

Consider these two hands:

OPENER	RESPONDER
♠ A K 10 8 7 5	♠ Q J 3
♥ 9 8 2	♥ J 7 3
♦ K 4	♦ A Q J 10 8 3
♣ A K	♣ Q

OPENER	RESPONDER
1♠	2♦
2♠	3♠
?	

After responder raises to 3♠, the trump suit has been agreed. Opener has enough strength to take the partnership to slam, but using Blackwood right now won't help. Responder will show one ace, and whether opener stops in 5♠ or continues to 6♠, the partnership is too high. The defenders can take the first three heart tricks.

Before taking over the captaincy and using Blackwood, opener should be reasonably sure the partnership has at least second-round control in every suit. Opener knows that's the case in spades, diamonds, and clubs, but needs to find out whether responder has either first- or second-round control in hearts. So opener initiates a control-showing sequence:

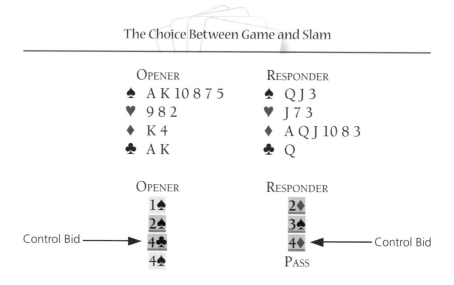

OPENER | RESPONDER
♠ A K 10 8 7 5 | ♠ Q J 3
♥ 9 8 2 | ♥ J 7 3
♦ K 4 | ♦ A Q J 10 8 3
♣ A K | ♣ Q

OPENER | RESPONDER
1♠ | 2♦
2♠ | 3♠
Control Bid ⟶ 4♣ | 4♦ ⟵ Control Bid
4♠ | PASS

With no interest in slam, opener would simply bid 4♠ once spades have been agreed upon. So opener's 4♣ bid is a control-showing bid. Responder cooperates with a control-showing bid of 4♦. Opener doesn't have a control in the heart suit, so opener returns to the agreed trump suit, 4♠. Responder also doesn't have a control in the heart suit and doesn't want to venture beyond game, so responder passes and the partnership stops safely at the game level.

How does responder know that opener's 4♠ bid isn't a further control-showing bid? The partnership needs a way to stop below slam when it doesn't have the required controls, so the trump suit is not included when showing controls[34]. A return to the trump suit says, "I have nothing further to show." It doesn't necessarily end the auction. Partner may still have more to say, but it does allow the partnership to stop in a game contract.

---

[34] Key Card Blackwood, discussed in Appendix 8, can be used to find out about controls in the trump suit.

There are other ways the partnership can stop the control-showing process. With enough information, either player may simply jump to the slam level. Or either player may employ the Blackwood convention by bidding 4NT.

STOPPING THE CONTROL-SHOWING PROCESS

The partnership can stop the control-showing process by:

- Returning to the agreed trump suit.
- Jumping to slam.
- Bidding Blackwood.

Why use Blackwood after the partnership has been showing controls?

- Controls in the trump suit are not included in the control-showing process. Blackwood may still be needed to confirm that the partnership has enough controls.
- There may be ambiguity between first- and second-round controls. Blackwood can be used to clarify the situation.

Let's modify the previous hands:

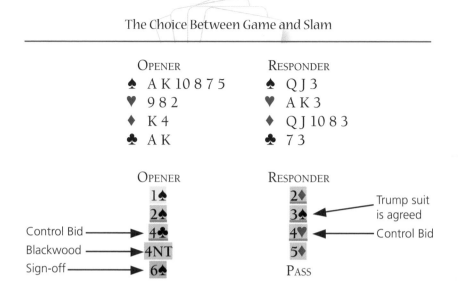

After the trump suit has been agreed with responder's raise to 3♠, opener makes a move toward slam with the 4♣ bid. Responder cooperates by bidding 4♥. That's exactly what opener wanted to hear. There's no longer a concern that the opponents can take the first two heart tricks, so opener bids Blackwood to confirm that the partnership isn't missing two aces, and confidently takes the partnership to slam when responder shows an ace.

Control-showing bids followed by Blackwood will often work when an early jump to Blackwood needs to be avoided.

Guidelines for Showing Controls

The control-showing process can be challenging, and requires both partners to be on the same wavelength. Here are some useful guidelines:

- Once the control-showing process is initiated, partner is expected to cooperate below the game level, even with a minimum hand.
- Controls are rarely shown if they take the partnership beyond game.
- Both first- and second-round controls can be shown.
- Controls are typically shown 'up the line.'
- Controls are not shown in the agreed trump suit. Blackwood must be used to check on the total number of aces and kings held by the partnership.

COOPERATION

If partner makes a move toward slam with a control-showing bid, do we have to cooperate? Obviously if we have extra values, we want to help get to slam. We might even take charge and use Blackwood. After all, if partner is interested in slam and we are also interested, what's stopping us? If we don't have extra values, however, do we have to make a control-showing bid once partner starts the process? In general, we cooperate with partner below the game level when we have something useful to show, even when we have no extra values.

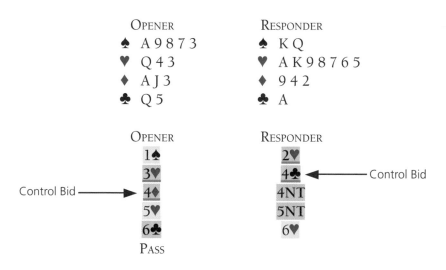

	OPENER		RESPONDER
♠	A 9 8 7 3	♠	K Q
♥	Q 4 3	♥	A K 9 8 7 6 5
♦	A J 3	♦	9 4 2
♣	Q 5	♣	A

	OPENER	RESPONDER	
	1♠	2♥	
	3♥	4♣	← Control Bid
Control Bid →	4♦	4NT	
	5♥	5NT	
	6♣	6♥	
	PASS		

After the partnership agrees on hearts as the trump suit, responder shows interest in slam with a control-showing bid of 4♣. Although opener has no extra values, showing the ♦A doesn't take the partnership beyond game. It turns out that a diamond control is exactly what responder is looking for. Now responder can safely use Blackwood to check for aces. When the partnership has all the aces, responder can even make a try for grand slam by asking about kings. When opener shows no kings, responder settles for a small slam.

AVOID CONTROL-BIDDING BEYOND GAME

With rare exceptions[35], we avoid making a control-showing bid that takes the partnership past game. When bidding beyond game, the default action is to bid Blackwood and check for aces and kings.

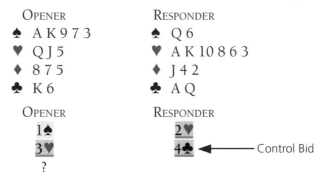

OPENER	RESPONDER
♠ A K 9 7 3	♠ Q 6
♥ Q J 5	♥ A K 10 8 6 3
♦ 8 7 5	♦ J 4 2
♣ K 6	♣ A Q

OPENER	RESPONDER
1♠	2♥
3♥	4♣ ◄——— Control Bid
?	

If opener continues the control-showing process by bidding 4♠, the partnership will get too high. So opener simply returns to 4♥, leaving any further move to responder. Here, responder passes, knowing the partnership doesn't have a control in diamonds.

OPENER	RESPONDER
♠ A J 10 8 7 6	♠ K Q 5
♥ A Q	♥ K 9 8 6 3
♦ J 3 2	♦ 5
♣ Q 5	♣ A K J 6

OPENER	RESPONDER
1♠	2♥
2♠	3♠
Control Bid ——► 4♥	?

After spades have been agreed and opener shows the control in hearts, responder might be tempted to continue the control-showing process with a bid of 5♣. However, when opener now bids 5♠, responder has no idea whether to bid slam. Opener might not have the ♠A, and the partnership could be missing the ♠A and ♦A. Instead, responder should simply bid Blackwood over 4♥. When opener shows two aces, responder can bid 6♠.

[35] Appendix 9 provides examples of showing controls beyond the game level.

SHOWING FIRST- AND SECOND-ROUND CONTROLS

Although some partnerships prefer to always show first-round controls ahead of second-round controls, this wastes space, especially if a second-round control could be shown below game, while showing a first-round control would go beyond the security of game. It is generally safe to show a second-round control below game, because Blackwood is still available to check that the partnership isn't missing too many aces.

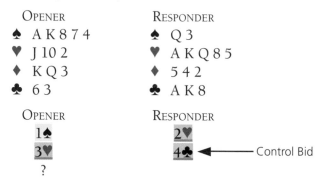

OPENER	RESPONDER
♠ A K 8 7 4	♠ Q 3
♥ J 10 2	♥ A K Q 8 5
♦ K Q 3	♦ 5 4 2
♣ 6 3	♣ A K 8

OPENER	RESPONDER	
1♠	2♥	
3♥	4♣	◄——— Control Bid
?		

After hearts have been agreed and responder shows a control in clubs, opener has to decide what to do. A bid of 4♠ would take the partnership beyond 4♥, so opener doesn't want to do that with a minimum hand. However, if opener simply bids 4♥, responder will be worried about diamonds and will likely pass.

The auction is smoother if opener shows the diamond control:

	OPENER	RESPONDER	
	1♠	2♥	
	3♥	4♣	◄——— Control Bid
Control Bid ——►	4♦	4NT	
	5♦	6♥	
	PASS		

Once opener shows a control in diamonds, responder can confidently bid Blackwood to check for aces, knowing the opponents won't take the first two diamond tricks. Responder isn't too concerned that the partnership might be missing both first- and second-round control in spades, since that is opener's first suit.

The partnership can also reach the slam if opener's second-round control in diamonds is a singleton instead of the ♦K.

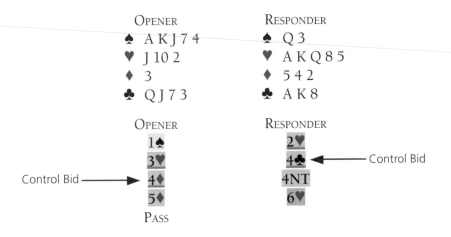

	OPENER	RESPONDER
♠	A K J 7 4	Q 3
♥	J 10 2	A K Q 8 5
♦	3	5 4 2
♣	Q J 7 3	A K 8

OPENER	RESPONDER
1♠	2♥
3♥	4♣ ← Control Bid
Control Bid → 4♦	4NT
5♦	6♥
PASS	

If the partnership has agreed to show both first- and second-round controls below the level of game, then bypassing a suit during a control-showing sequence denies a control in that suit. That would keep the partnership out of trouble if these were the combined hands:

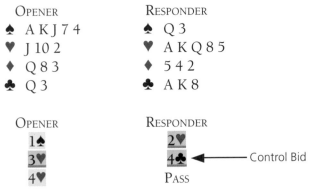

	OPENER	RESPONDER
♠	A K J 7 4	Q 3
♥	J 10 2	A K Q 8 5
♦	Q 8 3	5 4 2
♣	Q 3	A K 8

OPENER	RESPONDER
1♠	2♥
3♥	4♣ ← Control Bid
4♥	PASS

By going back to the agreed trump suit over responder's 4♣ bid, opener denies either first- or second-round control of diamonds. Responder isn't tempted to bid any more, which is a good thing. The defenders may be able to take the first three diamond tricks.

SHOWING CONTROLS 'UP THE LINE'

Controls are usually shown 'up the line'—cheapest first. This helps conserve bidding space and allows partner to draw inferences when a suit is bypassed.

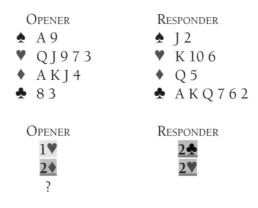

OPENER	RESPONDER
♠ A 9	♠ J 2
♥ Q J 9 7 3	♥ K 10 6
♦ A K J 4	♦ Q 5
♣ 8 3	♣ A K Q 7 6 2

OPENER	RESPONDER
1♥	2♣
2♦	2♥
?	

Once responder bids 2♥, the trump suit has been agreed. With extra values, opener wants to show interest in slam and has a choice between showing the ♠A or ♦A. Suppose opener were to start with showing the ♦A by bidding diamonds at the three level:

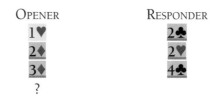

OPENER	RESPONDER
1♥	2♣
2♦	2♥
3♦	4♣
?	

Now it becomes awkward to show the ♠A, since that would take the partnership beyond game. Opener doesn't have enough extra strength to take over and bid Blackwood. If opener bids 4♥, however, responder can't go any higher with nothing in spades.

It is much more efficient if opener starts showing controls as cheaply as possible:

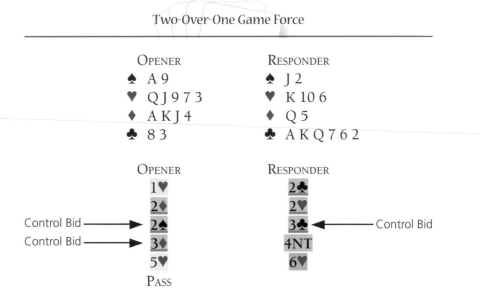

OPENER	RESPONDER
♠ A 9	♠ J 2
♥ Q J 9 7 3	♥ K 10 6
♦ A K J 4	♦ Q 5
♣ 8 3	♣ A K Q 7 6 2

	OPENER	RESPONDER	
	1♥	2♣	
	2♦	2♥	
Control Bid →	2♠	3♣	← Control Bid
Control Bid →	3♦	4NT	
	5♥	6♥	
	PASS		

By going up the line, opener has shown both the ♠A and ♦A by the time the auction is at only 3♦. There's plenty of room left for further investigation below game, although by now responder knows opener has spades covered and can take charge, using Blackwood to check on the total number of aces before bidding to slam.

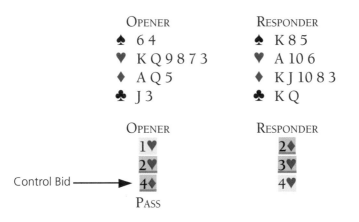

OPENER	RESPONDER
♠ 6 4	♠ K 8 5
♥ K Q 9 8 7 3	♥ A 10 6
♦ A Q 5	♦ K J 10 8 3
♣ J 3	♣ K Q

	OPENER	RESPONDER
	1♥	2♦
	2♥	3♥
Control Bid →	4♦	4♥
	PASS	

After hearts are agreed, opener expresses interest in slam by making a control-showing bid of 4♦. Responder has a lot of extra values, but can draw the inference that opener has neither the ♠A nor ♣A, since opener bypassed both suits. Responder settles for game.

Control-Showing or Blackwood?

Let's revisit those earlier hands where a premature use of Blackwood could lead to a problem and see how this can be resolved with the help of the control-showing process.

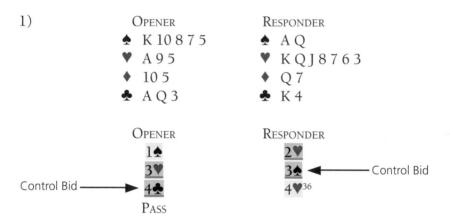

1)

	OPENER	RESPONDER
♠	K 10 8 7 5	♠ A Q
♥	A 9 5	♥ K Q J 8 7 6 3
♦	10 5	♦ Q 7
♣	A Q 3	♣ K 4

	OPENER	RESPONDER	
	1♠	2♥	
	3♥	3♠ ◄———— Control Bid
Control Bid ———►	4♣	4♥³⁶	
	PASS		

After hearts are agreed upon as the trump suit, responder has enough strength to want to go to slam, but should avoid using Blackwood without a control in the unbid diamond suit. So responder starts the slam exploration with a control-showing bid of 3♠. When neither responder nor opener can show a control in the diamond suit, the partnership can stop before getting to the slam level.

---

[36] Even if responder makes a further try with 4♠ rather than stopping in 4♥, the partnership will stop below the slam level when opener bids 5♥.

---

2)

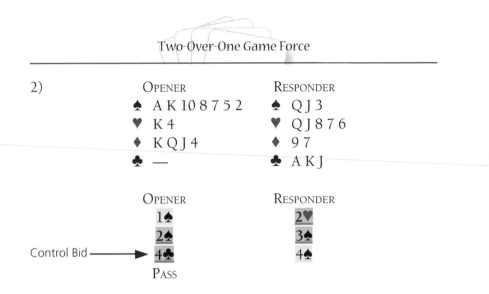

	OPENER	RESPONDER
	♠ A K 10 8 7 5 2	♠ Q J 3
	♥ K 4	♥ Q J 8 7 6
	♦ K Q J 4	♦ 9 7
	♣ —	♣ A K J

	OPENER	RESPONDER
	1♠	2♥
	2♠	3♠
Control Bid ⟶	4♣	4♠
	PASS	

Opener has enough that slam is likely, but Blackwood should be avoided because of the void in clubs. If responder shows only one ace, opener won't know what to do. Instead, opener wants to know about specific aces, the ♦A and ♥A. The way to find that information is through the control-showing process.

Opener shows the first-round control in clubs, the club void, with a bid of 4♣. Responder, looking at the ♣A and ♣K, may be a little surprised that opener is showing a control in clubs! But responder can figure out that opener must have a void or singleton in clubs. With no control in either diamonds or hearts, responder simply returns to spades, the agreed trump suit. Opener, trusting that responder has neither the ♦A nor the ♥A, reluctantly settles for game.

3)

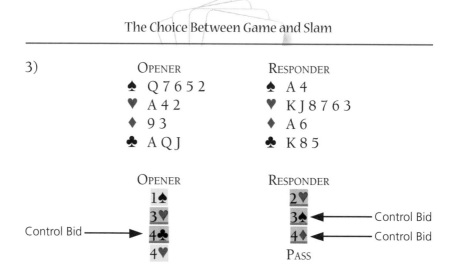

OPENER	RESPONDER
♠ Q 7 6 5 2	♠ A 4
♥ A 4 2	♥ K J 8 7 6 3
♦ 9 3	♦ A 6
♣ A Q J	♣ K 8 5

OPENER	RESPONDER	
1♠	2♥	
3♥	3♠	◄——— Control Bid
Control Bid ——► 4♣	4♦	◄——— Control Bid
4♥	PASS	

The problem here is that responder isn't strong enough to assume the captaincy and bid Blackwood. Instead, responder shows interest in slam with the 3♠ bid, and opener cooperates by bidding 4♣ to show the ♣A. Responder shows further interest by bidding 4♦, but with no extra values, opener goes back to the agreed trump suit. Responder has given slam a couple of tries, but that's enough. The partnership rests safely in game. The partnership has controls in every suit, but not enough combined strength for slam.

The Principle of Fast Arrival

One of the major advantages of 2/1 Game Force is that it allows the partnership to take its time exploring for the best contract, and deciding whether there is enough extra strength to consider a slam. Neither partner is worried about a bid being passed below the game level. So why would either player jump to game after a 2/1 response and use up some of the extra bidding room? It has to do with the *principle of fast arrival*:

PRINCIPLE OF FAST ARRIVAL

When the partnership has found a fit and is committed to the game level:

- Bidding **quickly** to game shows no interest in slam.
- Bidding **slowly** toward game shows interest in slam.

If we know How High and Where the partnership belongs, we should get there directly before something goes wrong. "The one who knows...goes!"

One advantage of going directly to game without making any 'extra' bids is that it gives less information to the opponents. They may not get off to the best opening lead, and they may have difficulty finding the best defense thereafter. There is also the preemptive factor. Jumping right to game makes it tougher for the opponents to come into the auction with an overcall or double.

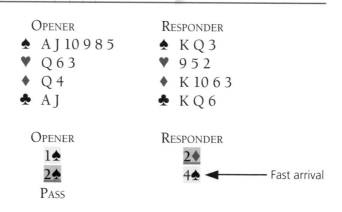

OPENER	RESPONDER
♠ A J 10 9 8 5	♠ K Q 3
♥ Q 6 3	♥ 9 5 2
♦ Q 4	♦ K 10 6 3
♣ A J	♣ K Q 6

OPENER	RESPONDER	
1♠	2♦	
2♠	4♠ ◄─────── Fast arrival	
PASS		

After the 1♠ opening, the 2♦ response commits the partnership to the game level. Opener has some extra values, but simply shows the extra length by rebidding the suit.

At this point, responder knows WHERE the partnership belongs, spades. With a minimum for the 2/1 response, 13 points, responder also knows HOW HIGH, game. Unless opener has considerable extra values, slam is unlikely. Using the principle of fast arrival, responder wastes no more time and jumps directly to game.

This has two advantages. Opener would like to bid more, but is warned by the jump to game that responder has no interest in slam. The partnership does well to stop in game, since slam has no chance, and even game is uncertain. The opponents might be able to take the first three heart tricks and the ♦A to defeat 4♠. That's the second advantage of responder's jump. It gives no further information to the defenders. If they lead a club rather than a heart, game is assured. Declarer can discard a heart on the extra club winner.

What if responder held a stronger hand?

OPENER	RESPONDER
♠ A J 10 9 8 5	♠ K Q 3
♥ Q 6 3	♥ K J 5
♦ Q 4	♦ A K J 10 6
♣ A J	♣ 6 5

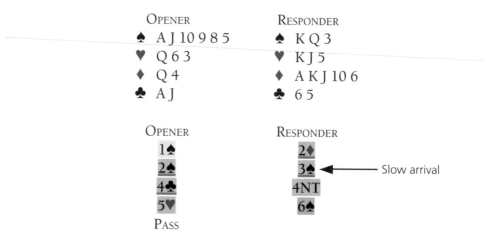

OPENER	RESPONDER	
1♠	2♦	
2♠	3♠	← Slow arrival
4♣	4NT	
5♥	6♠	
PASS		

The auction starts the same way, but after opener's 2♠ rebid, responder takes the 'slow' approach by raising to 3♠, taking advantage of the 2/1 Game Force. Responder knows WHERE the contract belongs, spades, but is not sure How HIGH. Responder has enough extra strength that slam is a possibility.

Over responder's raise to 3♠, opener is happy to have the opportunity to cooperate in looking for slam. Opener makes a control-showing bid of 4♣, and the partnership is on its way. The partnership reaches the excellent 6♠ contract.

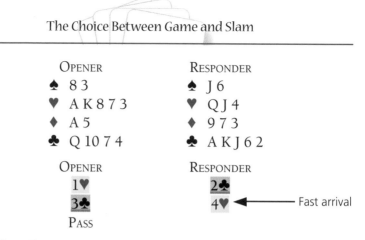

OPENER
♠ 8 3
♥ A K 8 7 3
♦ A 5
♣ Q 10 7 4

RESPONDER
♠ J 6
♥ Q J 4
♦ 9 7 3
♣ A K J 6 2

OPENER	RESPONDER
1♥	2♣
3♣	4♥ ◄────── Fast arrival
PASS	

After the 1♥ opening, responder knows there is an eight-card fit and is planning to take the partnership to 4♥. However, an immediate jump to 4♥ would be preemptive, and responder can't make some form of forcing raise, such as Jacoby 2NT, with only three-card support. So responder 'temporizes' by bidding a new suit, with no intention of actually playing in clubs. After opener raises clubs, responder follows through with the plan to get to game in hearts. The jump to 4♥ tells opener that responder has a minimum for the 2/1 response, and little interest in slam. Opener passes happily.

Let's give responder a better hand:

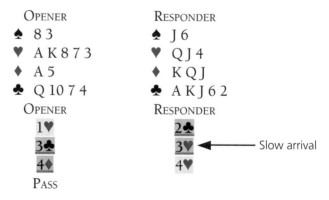

OPENER
♠ 8 3
♥ A K 8 7 3
♦ A 5
♣ Q 10 7 4

RESPONDER
♠ J 6
♥ Q J 4
♦ K Q J
♣ A K J 6 2

OPENER	RESPONDER
1♥	2♣
3♣	3♥ ◄────── Slow arrival
4♦	4♥
PASS	

Now responder bids only 3♥, leaving lots of room to explore for slam. Opener cooperates by bidding 4♦. Responder is worried about spades, however, and can't afford to venture beyond game. Opener also has nothing in spades, so the partnership stops at the game level, but at least the possibility of slam was investigated.

WHEN TO USE FAST ARRIVAL

Bidding space can be valuable, especially when the partnership needs to use control-showing bids to investigate slam. So fast arrival should be used only with a minimum hand and poor slam values. A weak trump holding and stray queens and jacks are usually poor values for slam. Aces, kings, singletons, and voids, are prime values.

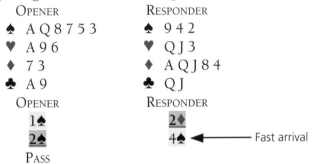

OPENER	RESPONDER
♠ A Q 8 7 5 3	♠ 9 4 2
♥ A 9 6	♥ Q J 3
♦ 7 3	♦ A Q J 8 4
♣ A 9	♣ Q J

OPENER	RESPONDER
1♠	2♦
2♠	4♠ ◄——— Fast arrival
PASS	

Responder's hand is unsuitable for slam after opener rebids 2♠. The trump support is poor, and the side suits consist of queens and jacks. So responder uses fast arrival, and the partnership stops in game.

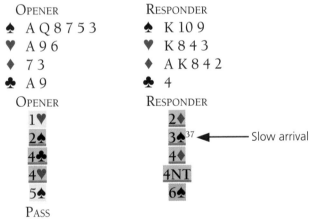

OPENER	RESPONDER
♠ A Q 8 7 5 3	♠ K 10 9
♥ A 9 6	♥ K 8 4 3
♦ 7 3	♦ A K 8 4 2
♣ A 9	♣ 4

OPENER	RESPONDER
1♥	2♦
2♠	3♠[37] ◄——— Slow arrival
4♣	4♦
4♥	4NT
5♠	6♠
PASS	

Responder's excellent trump support and wealth of controls make this hand too strong to settle for game. Once opener also shows interest in slam, the partnership is on its way. Even a grand slam might make if declarer can establish an extra diamond winner!

---

[37] Responder might make a splinter bid of 4♣ if that is part of the partnership methods.

FAST ARRIVAL IS NOT A SIGNOFF

Fast arrival does not rule out the possibility of slam when partner has extra values.

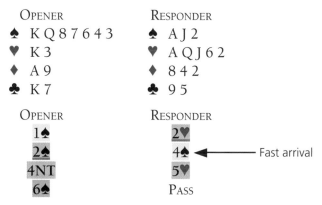

Opener	Responder
♠ K Q 8 7 6 4 3	♠ A J 2
♥ K 3	♥ A Q J 6 2
♦ A 9	♦ 8 4 2
♣ K 7	♣ 9 5

Opener	Responder	
1♠	2♥	
2♠	4♠	◄———— Fast arrival
4NT	5♥	
6♠	Pass	

With a minimum for the 2/1 response, responder jumps to game over the 2♠ rebid. That doesn't deter opener from going to slam once responder shows a fit for spades, along with enough strength for a 2/1 game-forcing response.

OPENER'S FAST ARRIVAL

In some auctions, opener can use fast arrival to show a minimum hand:

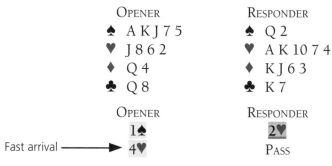

Opener	Responder
♠ A K J 7 5	♠ Q 2
♥ J 8 6 2	♥ A K 10 7 4
♦ Q 4	♦ K J 6 3
♣ Q 8	♣ K 7

	Opener	Responder
	1♠	2♥
Fast arrival ———►	4♥	Pass

Opener likes the 2♥ response, but has a minimum opening bid and no controls in the unbid suits. Opener quickly takes the partnership to game. Responder knows that opener could have simply raised to 3♥ to leave more room for slam exploration. So if opener isn't interested in slam, neither is responder.

Conclusion

The two adaptations to standard methods that are needed to use 2/1 Game Force are quite straightforward:

- A 2/1 response is a marathon bid.
- A 1NT response to 1♥ or 1♠ is forcing for one round.

In addition, these changes only apply if responder is an unpassed hand, and if responder's right-hand opponent passes. What could be simpler?

Nonetheless, the impact can be significant. By leaving more bidding room after the 2/1 response, the partnership can use the extra space to explore for the best game contract and to investigate the possibility of a slam. The partnership is still free to use any of its other favorite conventions and agreements. A win-win situation!

Summary

HOW HIGH: GAME OR SLAM?

Once the partnership has agreed **WHERE** the contract is to be played, it can focus on **HOW HIGH**. Three factors to bear in mind when considering slam are:

- Combined strength: The partnership needs about 33 points—or a reasonable expectation of taking twelve tricks—for a small slam and 37 for a grand slam.
- Fit: Only with a suitable trump fit can distributional features such as singletons and voids come into play.
- Controls: First-round control in three suits and at least second-round control in the fourth are needed for a small slam. A grand slam requires first-round control in every suit.

FINDING OUT ABOUT CONTROLS

The Blackwood convention is used to discover **how many** aces and/or kings partner holds. However, control-bidding should be used when:

- Holding only low cards in an unbid suit.
- Holding a void.
- Inviting slam.

CONTROL BIDDING

Once the trump suit has been agreed, the bid of another suit is a control-showing bid, showing interest in slam.

- The control-showing process rarely continues beyond the game level.
- Both first-round controls—aces and voids—and second-round controls—kings and singletons—can be shown.
- With a choice of controls to show, controls are usually bid 'up the line', leaving the maximum amount of room.
- Controls are not shown in the trump suit itself.
- The partnership can stop the control-showing process by returning to the agreed trump suit, jumping to slam, or bidding Blackwood.

PRINCIPLE OF FAST ARRIVAL

When the partnership has found a fit and is committed to the game level:

- Bidding **quickly** to game shows no interest in slam.
- Bidding **slowly** toward game shows interest in slam.

Quiz – Part I

North opens 1♠, South responds 2♥, and North raises to 3♥. What does South, responder, bid next with each of the following hands?

West	North	East	South	
	1♠	Pass	2♥	NORTH
Pass	3♥	Pass	?	WEST — EAST
				SOUTH

a) ♠ Q 7
♥ K Q 8 6 2
♦ 10 3
♣ K Q J 6

b) ♠ K 5
♥ K Q 9 8 7 3 2
♦ 4
♣ A K J

c) ♠ 9 5
♥ A K J 8 3
♦ K 4
♣ A J 8 5

d) ♠ Q 3
♥ A K Q 7 6 5
♦ K Q J 4 2
♣ —

e) ♠ 5 3
♥ A Q 9 7 3
♦ A K J
♣ Q 9 5

f) ♠ 8 6
♥ K Q 8 6 3
♦ A Q
♣ A J 8 7

South opens 1♠, North responds 2♥, South raises to 3♥, and North bids 4♣. What does South, opener, bid next?

West	North	East	South	
			1♠	NORTH
Pass	2♥	Pass	3♥	WEST — EAST
Pass	4♣	Pass	?	SOUTH

g) ♠ K J 9 7 5
♥ A J 8
♦ J 4
♣ K 8 3

h) ♠ A Q 9 7 3
♥ Q 8 3
♦ A J 8
♣ 7 4

i) ♠ A Q 8 5 3
♥ K J 6 3
♦ A K
♣ 8 3

j) ♠ K 10 8 7 5 3
♥ A Q 8
♦ K Q
♣ Q 4

k) ♠ A K 9 7 3
♥ K Q 6
♦ 5
♣ K J 8 2

l) ♠ A J 10 7 3
♥ K 10 8 3
♦ —
♣ K J 7 5

Answers to Quiz – Part I

a) 4♥. Now that the trump suit has been agreed upon, responder can simply bid game. With no extra values, responder has no interest in slam. Any move in that direction will have to come from opener.

b) 4NT. Responder has enough extra strength that slam is possible, provided the partnership isn't missing two aces. If opener shows one ace, responder will stop in 5♥; if opener has two aces, responder will bid 6♥; if opener has three aces, responder can go for a grand slam.

c) 4♣. Once the fit is found, responder has some interest in slam, but not enough strength to take control and bid Blackwood. Instead, responder expresses interest by making a control-showing bid of 4♣.

d) 4♣ (6♥). Blackwood won't be helpful here. If opener shows one ace, responder still won't know what to do. Holding a void, responder can make a control-showing bid of 4♣. Hopefully opener can now show a first-round control in either diamonds or spades. Second choice is for responder to simply jump to 6♥ and hope for the best.

e) 4♦. With no first- or second-round control in clubs, responder can't immediately use Blackwood. Instead, responder can show a control in diamonds, looking for help from opener.

f) 4♣. With interest in slam and first-round control in both clubs and diamonds, responder bids 4♣, showing controls up the line.

g) 4♥. Responder is showing interest in slam with the 4♣ bid. With nothing extra to show, opener returns to the agreed trump suit.

h) 4♦. Opener can cooperate with responder's slam try by showing the ♦A. That might be just the thing responder needs to know about.

i) 4NT (4♦). Opener could make a control-showing bid of 4♦, but with this much extra strength and responder showing slam interest, opener can simply take over and use Blackwood.

j) 4♦. Bidding 4♥ would deny a control in diamonds. So opener should show the second-round control.

k) 4NT. Opener could continue showing controls, but with a singleton diamond, knows that the partnership has a first- or second-round control in every suit. Opener can use Blackwood to check for aces.

l) 4♦. A void serves the same purpose as an ace in a trump contract. So opener continues the control-showing process by bidding 4♦.

Quiz – Part II

What call does South make with the given hand in each of the following auctions?

a)

WEST	NORTH	EAST	SOUTH	
			1♥	♠ Q 7 3
				♥ A K J 8 6
PASS	2♣	PASS	2NT	♦ A J 4
PASS	3NT	PASS	?	♣ Q 4

b)

WEST	NORTH	EAST	SOUTH	
		PASS	1♠	♠ A Q J 8 3
				♥ K 9 5
PASS	2♥	PASS	3♥	♦ Q 10 6 2
PASS	4♣	PASS	?	♣ 7

c)

WEST	NORTH	EAST	SOUTH	
			1♠	♠ A Q J 7 6 2
				♥ Q 7
PASS	2♦	PASS	2♠	♦ K 4
PASS	3♠	PASS	4♣	♣ A J 5
PASS	4♠	PASS	?	

d)

WEST	NORTH	EAST	SOUTH	
	1♥	PASS	2♦	♠ A K 7
				♥ Q 5
PASS	2NT	PASS	?	♦ A Q 10 8 3
				♣ A 5 4

e)

WEST	NORTH	EAST	SOUTH	
	1♠	PASS	2♦	♠ 4
				♥ 9 4
PASS	2♥	PASS	3♦	♦ A K J 8 7 6 3
PASS	3♥	PASS	?	♣ K Q J

f)

WEST	NORTH	EAST	SOUTH	
	1♠	PASS	2♥	♠ A 6 4
				♥ K Q 8 7 3 2
PASS	2♠	PASS	3♠	♦ 6
PASS	4♣	PASS	?	♣ Q 9 5

Answers to Quiz – Part II

a) 4NT. With 18 points—17 high-card points plus 1 length point for the five-card suit—opener has enough to invite partner to slam in notrump. Opener is showing about 18-19 points, too much to open 1NT. Responder can pass with a minimum or continue to slam with a little extra.

b) 4♥. Since hearts have been agreed, responder is showing slam interest with the 4♣ bid. However, opener has no first- or second-round control in diamonds and would have to go beyond game to show the control in spades. Without enough strength to assume the captaincy and bid Blackwood, opener should simply return to the agreed trump suit.

c) **Pass**. Opener has enough strength that slam is likely, but avoids Blackwood with no control in hearts, one of the unbid suits. So opener starts a control-showing sequence by bidding 4♣. Responder returns to the trump suit, bypassing both diamonds and hearts. So responder has denied a control in either suit and opener has to settle for game.

d) 6NT. With 19 high-card points plus 1 length point for the five-card diamond suit, responder has enough to take the partnership to slam in notrump when opener shows a balanced hand. If opener has 18 or 19 rather than 12–14, opener can continue to 7NT.

e) 3NT. Responder has some interest in slam, but the partnership hands don't appear to fit together very well. Responder will have to settle in 3NT for now. Opener can still bid again with extra strength or more distribution.

f) 4♦. Opener has started a control-showing sequence now that spades have been agreed upon as the trump suit. Responder can cooperate by showing a control in diamonds. A singleton serves as a second-round control. With controls in both diamonds and hearts, responder bids up the line.

Quiz – Part III

What call does South make in each of the following auctions?

a)	WEST	NORTH	EAST	SOUTH	♠ A K Q 8 5
			PASS	1♠	♥ Q J 7
	PASS	2♥	PASS	3♥	♦ K Q 6
	PASS	4NT	PASS	5♦	♣ 10 4
	PASS	5♥	PASS	?	

b)	WEST	NORTH	EAST	SOUTH	♠ A Q J 7 3
			PASS	1♠	♥ 8 4
	PASS	2♣	PASS	2♦	♦ K Q 9 6
	PASS	2♠	PASS	?	♣ 7 4

c)	WEST	NORTH	EAST	SOUTH	♠ Q 6 2
		1♠	PASS	2♦	♥ Q 5
	PASS	2♣	PASS	3♠	♦ A Q J 8 3
	PASS	4♣	PASS	4♦	♣ K Q 5
	PASS	4♠	PASS	?	

d)	WEST	NORTH	EAST	SOUTH	♠ 3
		1♠	PASS	2♥	♥ A K 9 8 7 3 2
	PASS	3♥	PASS	4♣	♦ 9 4
	PASS	4♦	PASS	4NT	♣ A K Q
	PASS	5♥	PASS	?	

e)	WEST	NORTH	EAST	SOUTH	♠ Q 4
		1♥	PASS	2♣	♥ K J 3
	PASS	2♥	PASS	?	♦ 8 6
					♣ K Q 8 7 6 3

f)	WEST	NORTH	EAST	SOUTH	♠ A 7
		1♠	PASS	2♦	♥ 5 2
	PASS	2♠	PASS	?	♦ A Q J 8 3
					♣ A 10 8 3

Answers to Quiz – Part III

a) **Pass**. Even though opener has extra values and responder has shown interest in slam by bidding Blackwood, opener should not override responder's decision to stop in 5♥. Responder knows how many aces the partnership holds; opener does not.

b) **4♠**. With nothing extra for slam purposes, opener can follow the principle of fast arrival once responder has shown the spade fit, and simply jump to game. Responder can bid again with a very strong hand, but otherwise, why give more information to the defenders?

c) **Pass**. Opener showed slam interest with the 4♣ bid and responder cooperated with the 4♦ bid. However, when opener returns to the agreed trump suit, it sounds as though opener doesn't have a control in hearts. Neither does responder. So the partnership will have to settle for game.

d) **5NT**. Now that responder knows the partnership has all the aces, why not go for a grand slam? If opener has a king, the partnership should have thirteen top tricks.

e) **4♥**. Responder always intended to take the partnership to game in hearts once partner opened 1♥. With nothing extra for the 2/1 response, responder can use the principle of fast arrival to take the partnership right to game, showing no interest in slam unless opener has a very strong hand.

f) **3♠**. Opener has shown at least six spades, so the partnership has an eight-card or longer major-suit fit. Responder can agree on spades by raising. With extra values, responder raises to only three spades—slow arrival—to leave room for slam exploration.

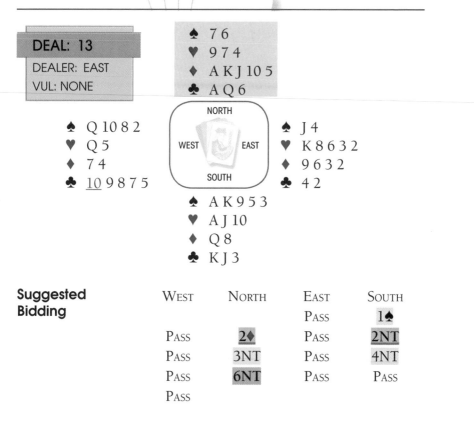

DEAL: 13
DEALER: EAST
VUL: NONE

♠ 7 6
♥ 9 7 4
♦ A K J 10 5
♣ A Q 6

♠ Q 10 8 2
♥ Q 5
♦ 7 4
♣ 10 9 8 7 5

♠ J 4
♥ K 8 6 3 2
♦ 9 6 3 2
♣ 4 2

♠ A K 9 5 3
♥ A J 10
♦ Q 8
♣ K J 3

Suggested Bidding	WEST	NORTH	EAST	SOUTH
			PASS	1♠
	PASS	2♦	PASS	2NT
	PASS	3NT	PASS	4NT
	PASS	6NT	PASS	PASS
	PASS			

East passes. South has 18 high-card points plus 1 length point for the five-card suit. The total of 19 points is too strong for 1NT but not strong enough for 2NT. South opens 1♠, and North makes a 2/1 response of 2♦. South now shows a balanced hand with the rebid of 2NT. There's no need to jump; the extra strength can be shown later. South wants to leave room for partner to make a further descriptive bid.

When North raises to 3NT, showing a willingness to play in notrump, South now shows the extra strength with a quantitative—invitational—raise to 4NT. This shows about 18-19 points. South would have passed with a minimum balanced hand of 12-14 points, or opened 1NT with 15-17 points. North has 14 high-card points plus 1 length point for the five-card suit, enough to accept the invitation.

Suggested Opening Lead

West can lead the ♣10, top of the solid sequence.

Suggested Play

Declarer has two sure spade tricks, a heart, five diamonds, and three clubs. That's eleven tricks; one more is needed. One possibility is the spade suit. If the missing spades are divided 3-3, declarer can develop two extra tricks through length. However, the odds of six outstanding cards dividing exactly 3-3 are about 35%, so declarer should look for a better alternative.

The heart suit offers a 75% chance for developing an extra trick. If East holds the ♥K, or ♥Q, or both the ♥K and ♥Q, declarer can develop an extra trick with the help of a repeated finesse. Only if West holds both the ♥K and ♥Q will the repeated finesse fail.

Declarer leads a low heart from dummy and finesses the ♥10. This first finesse loses to West's ♥Q. After regaining the lead, declarer can lead another low heart from dummy and finesse the ♥J. This finesse succeeds, and declarer has twelve tricks.

Declarer can't afford to give up a spade trick early, hoping that the suit will divide 3-3. When the spades prove to be divided 4-2, it's too late to try and develop an extra trick in hearts, since a trick must be lost in that suit.

Suggested Defense

If declarer plays five rounds of diamonds after winning the first trick, West must hold on to all four spades, unless declarer discards two or more spades. Otherwise, declarer will be able to establish a trick through length in spades. West knows from the auction that declarer has a five-card spade suit. West can afford to discard clubs—and even a low heart—if necessary.

If declarer plays on hearts rather than spades, there is nothing the defenders can do to prevent declarer from taking twelve tricks.

Conclusion

After a 2/1 game-forcing response, the partnership can focus first on WHERE and then on HOW HIGH. In quantitative auctions, both opener and responder can count points for length to reach the 33 combined points required for a small slam or 37 points for a grand slam. Either opener or responder can show extra strength by moving toward slam once the partnership has resolved WHERE to play the contract.

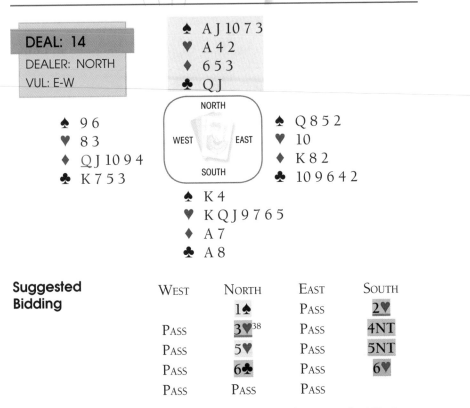

DEAL: 14

DEALER: NORTH

VUL: E-W

NORTH

♠ A J 10 7 3
♥ A 4 2
♦ 6 5 3
♣ Q J

WEST
♠ 9 6
♥ 8 3
♦ Q J 10 9 4
♣ K 7 5 3

EAST
♠ Q 8 5 2
♥ 10
♦ K 8 2
♣ 10 9 6 4 2

SOUTH
♠ K 4
♥ K Q J 9 7 6 5
♦ A 7
♣ A 8

Suggested Bidding

WEST	NORTH	EAST	SOUTH
	1♠	PASS	2♥
PASS	3♥[38]	PASS	4NT
PASS	5♥	PASS	5NT
PASS	6♣	PASS	6♥
PASS	PASS	PASS	

North opens the five-card spade suit, and South responds 2♥. Since South is promising a five-card or longer suit, North raises to 3♥, and the trump suit has been agreed.

South has 17 high-card points plus 3 length points for the seven-card suit. With 20 points opposite an opening bid, the partnership should have enough combined strength for slam. The only danger is that the partnership might be missing two aces. South uses Blackwood to check for the number of aces North holds. When North shows two, South can consider a grand slam and use 5NT to ask about kings. North's 6♣ response shows no kings, and South settles for a small slam.

Suggested Opening Lead

West would lead the ♦Q, top of the solid sequence, against the slam.

---

[38] North might apply the principle of fast arrival and jump to 4♥. However, South still has enough to use Blackwood.

Suggested Play

Declarer has eleven winners: two spades, seven hearts, the ♦A and ♣A. One more trick is needed. One possibility is the club finesse, but that's a 50-50 proposition. Declarer wants better odds than that.

The spade suit offers a couple of possibilities. The ♠Q might fall in two rounds, or the missing spades might divide 3-3. Declarer should at least plan to develop an extra spade trick before risking the club finesse. It would be nice if declarer could trump spades twice, since that would develop an extra trick even if the missing spades are divided 4-2. However, there is a shortage of entries to dummy. This plan won't work.

However, the presence of the ♠J-10 in dummy gives declarer a 100% play when the trumps are divided 2-1. Declarer wins the ♦A and draws two rounds of trumps with the ♥K-Q. Then declarer plays the ♠K and a spade to dummy's ♠A. When the ♠Q hasn't appeared, declarer leads the ♠J from dummy. If East plays the ♠Q, declarer can ruff, cross back to dummy with the ♥A, and discard a diamond on the ♠10 and a club on the last spade. If East doesn't play the ♠Q, or shows out, declarer discards the diamond loser on the ♠J—a *loser on a loser*. Even if West wins the ♠Q, the contract is secure. Declarer can use dummy's ♥A as an entry and discard a club on the ♠10. No need to risk taking the club finesse.

Suggested Defense

East should make an encouraging signal with the ♦8 on the first trick. If declarer tries the club finesse, West wins the ♣K and can lead another diamond to defeat the contract.

If declarer plays the ♠K, ♠A, and leads the ♠J from dummy, East should play a low spade. East knows declarer has no spades left, so playing the ♠Q will only establish dummy's ♠10 as a winner. If East plays low, declarer may choose to ruff the third round of spades. Now the contract can no longer be made. Declarer can't establish dummy's spades.

Conclusion

Once the trump suit has been agreed and one member of the partnership knows there is enough combined strength for a slam, the only remaining issue is whether the partnership has enough controls. If it is only necessary to know the number of aces and/or kings held by the partnership, the Blackwood convention can be used.

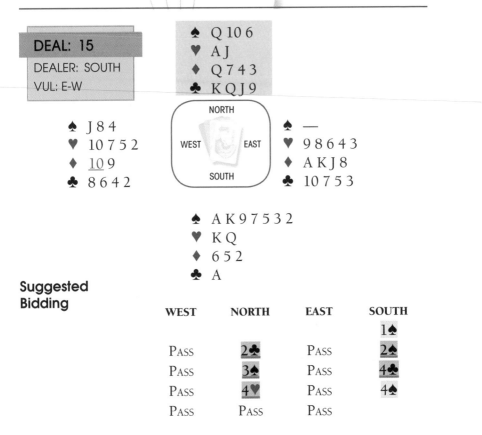

DEAL: 15

DEALER: SOUTH

VUL: E-W

NORTH

♠ Q 10 6
♥ A J
♦ Q 7 4 3
♣ K Q J 9

WEST

♠ J 8 4
♥ 10 7 5 2
♦ 10 9
♣ 8 6 4 2

EAST

♠ —
♥ 9 8 6 4 3
♦ A K J 8
♣ 10 7 5 3

SOUTH

♠ A K 9 7 5 3 2
♥ K Q
♦ 6 5 2
♣ A

Suggested Bidding

WEST	NORTH	EAST	SOUTH
			1♠
PASS	2♣	PASS	2♠
PASS	3♠	PASS	4♣
PASS	4♥	PASS	4♠
PASS	PASS	PASS	

South opens 1♠ and North makes a 2/1 response of 2♣. With two four-card suits, responder bids up the line. South's hand is worth 19 points—16 high-card points plus 3 length points for the seven-card suit. That's enough to consider a slam after responder shows enough to commit the partnership to game, but the initial focus is finding **WHERE** the partnership belongs. So South simply rebids the spade suit to show the extra length. After North raises to 3♠, the trump suit has been agreed, and South can now move toward slam.

The problem with using Blackwood to determine whether the partnership has enough aces is that if responder shows only one ace—as on this deal—South still won't know what to do. With no control in the diamond suit, South won't know whether the defenders can take the first two or three diamond tricks. Instead, South moves toward slam by making a control bid of 4♣.

North cooperates in the slam investigation by showing the ♥A. Since North bypassed diamonds, South is now sure that the partnership doesn't have a first- or second-round control in diamonds. So South bids 4♠, and the partnership stops short of slam.

Suggested Opening Lead

From listening to the auction, West can infer that North-South don't have first- or second-round control in diamonds and may choose to lead the ♦10, top of the doubleton, hoping to get a ruff.

Suggested Play

Suppose West leads the ♦10, and the defenders take the first three diamond tricks. East then leads a fourth round of diamonds. Declarer should be careful to ruff with the ♠K to avoid being overruffed. Having used one of the high trumps, declarer must still be careful in case the outstanding trumps are divided 3-0. Since East started with four diamonds and West with only two, West is more likely to hold the length in spades. So declarer should start with the ♠A. When East shows out on the first round of trumps, declarer can lead a low spade and finesse dummy's ♠10 to avoid losing a trump trick.

Suggested Defense

The defenders should always listen to the auction for clues for the best lead and best defense. If North-South use control-showing bids in the search for slam, it should be apparent that the best lead is a diamond. Starting with four rounds of diamonds is the best chance to defeat the contract.

What if South simply bids Blackwood and North-South reach a slam? Then West has a tough choice. If West leads anything other than a diamond, declarer can take all the tricks.

Conclusion

To uncover specific first- and second-round controls, the partnership has to go through a control-showing process. That's the only way to correctly avoid a slam on this deal. Blackwood should be avoided with no control in the diamond suit.

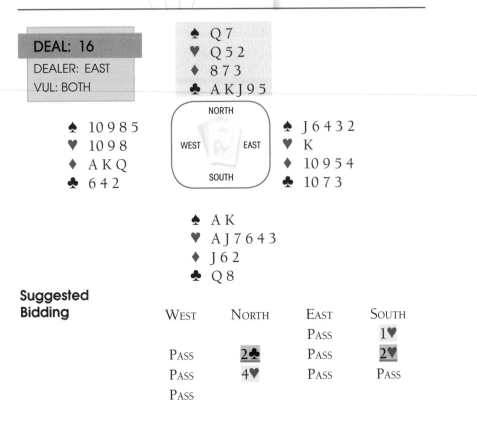

DEAL: 16

DEALER: EAST
VUL: BOTH

♠ Q 7
♥ Q 5 2
♦ 8 7 3
♣ A K J 9 5

♠ 10 9 8 5
♥ 10 9 8
♦ A K Q
♣ 6 4 2

♠ J 6 4 3 2
♥ K
♦ 10 9 5 4
♣ 10 7 3

♠ A K
♥ A J 7 6 4 3
♦ J 6 2
♣ Q 8

Suggested Bidding

WEST	NORTH	EAST	SOUTH
		PASS	1♥
PASS	2♣	PASS	2♥
PASS	4♥	PASS	PASS
PASS			

When South opens 1♥, North knows the partnership has at least an eight-card heart fit and enough combined strength for game. With only three-card support, North can't make an immediate forcing raise. Instead, North starts with a new suit response of 2♣. South's hand is worth 17 points—15 high-card points plus 2 length points—but there is no need to jump to show the extra strength after the 2/1 game-forcing response. South simply describes the extra length in hearts by rebidding the suit.

North can now show the heart suit. With a minimum 2/1 response and no interest in slam, North applies the principle of fast arrival and jumps right to 4♥. With interest in slam, North could simply raise to 3♥. South has extra values, but when North shows no interest in slam, South decides there's no reason to overrule North's judgment, and settles for game. The partnership avoids getting too high.

Suggested Opening Lead

West has an easy lead of the ♦A, top of the solid sequence.

Suggested Play

After the defenders take the first three diamond tricks, declarer has to take the rest. Missing the ♥K, declarer has to hope that East holds that card.

When playing the heart suit, declarer must be careful to lead a low heart from dummy, not the ♥Q. Declarer needs East to hold the singleton or doubleton ♥K to make the contract. Leading a low heart from dummy caters to both possibilities. Declarer can't make the contract if East has three or more hearts including the ♥K and defends correctly. If declarer leads the ♥Q, East can cover with the ♥K. Declarer can win the ♥A and ♥J, but will still have to lose to the remaining high heart.

The danger of leading the ♥Q is shown on the actual layout. South wins the ♥A, takes the ♥J, but has to lose a trick to West's ♥10. If declarer leads a low heart from dummy, East's ♥K pops up, and declarer doesn't have to lose a heart trick.

Suggested Defense

The defenders can't do anything if declarer handles the heart suit correctly. If East held three hearts, such as ♥K-9-8, East would have to cover if declarer led dummy's ♥Q in order to promote a heart trick when West holds the ♥10.

Conclusion

The quicker the partnership gets to game, the less the interest in slam. With slam interest, both partners want to go slowly to take advantage of the extra bidding room provided by the 2/1 Game Force agreement. The principle of fast arrival helps the partnership in a 2/1 auction when it comes to How High: Game or Slam.

Many roads lead to the Path, but basically there are only two: reason and practice.

—BODHIDHARMA, BUDDHIST MONK,
Fifth Century A.D.

Additional
Practice Deals

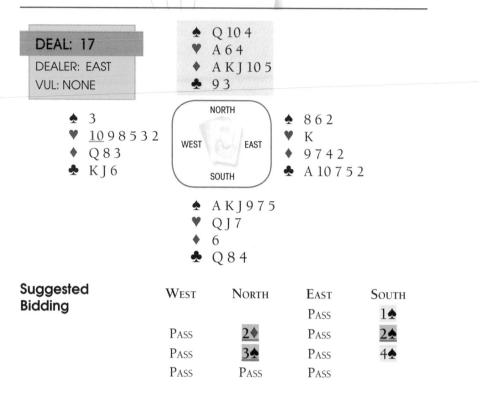

	WEST	NORTH	EAST	SOUTH
Suggested Bidding			PASS	1♠
	PASS	2♦	PASS	2♠
	PASS	3♠	PASS	4♠
	PASS	PASS	PASS	

Once South opens 1♠, North knows the partnership has at least an eight-card spade fit and enough combined strength for game. With only three-card support for spades, North starts with a new suit response of 2♦. After South rebids the spades, North agrees on spades as the trump suit by raising to 3♠.

With no extra values, South simply continues to 4♠. North doesn't have enough extra to consider going for a slam and is comfortable to settle for game.

Suggested Opening Lead

West would lead the ♥10, top of the solid sequence in hearts.

Suggested Play

Declarer can count six sure spade tricks, one heart trick, and two diamond tricks. A tenth trick can be developed through promotion in hearts. There is also the possibility of developing extra tricks from dummy's diamond suit, or perhaps trumping the third round of clubs in dummy.

With nine top tricks and a tenth that can be promoted in hearts, declarer doesn't need to take any chances. Declarer should play dummy's ♥A at trick one. When the ♥K falls under the ace, declarer will be rewarded with an overtrick[39]. There is no need to risk the contract by playing a low heart at trick one, hoping to win with the ♥J or ♥Q. The second heart winner can safely be promoted after trumps have been drawn.

Suggested Defense

If declarer plays low on the first heart, East wins the singleton ♥K, and now the defenders can defeat the contract. If East takes the ♣A and leads another club, West can win and lead a heart, which East can ruff.

East's best play after winning the ♥K is to play a low club at trick two. This might defeat the contract if declarer held the ♣K-J-6 instead of West. Declarer would have to decide whether to play the ♣K or ♣J. If declarer guessed to play the ♣J, West would win the ♣Q and could give East a heart ruff to defeat the contract. On the actual lie of the cards, a low club back could defeat the contract two tricks. If West immediately lead a heart for East to ruff, East could lead another low club to West, and get a second heart ruff.

Conclusion

Using 2/1 Game Force provides a comfortable way for responder to show a three-card forcing raise of opener's major suit, while leaving plenty of room for further exploration if either partner is interested in slam.

---

[39] Declarer can actually develop one or more additional tricks in the diamond suit to make more than one overtrick.

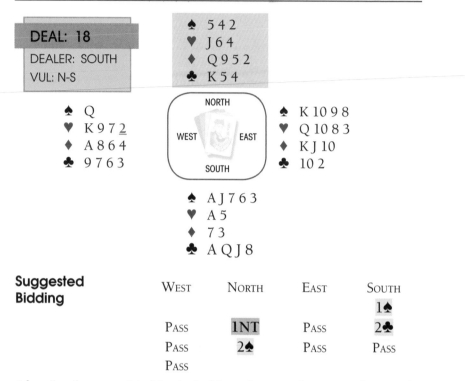

DEAL: 18

DEALER: SOUTH
VUL: N-S

♠ 5 4 2
♥ J 6 4
♦ Q 9 5 2
♣ K 5 4

NORTH

WEST   EAST

SOUTH

♠ Q
♥ K 9 7 2
♦ A 8 6 4
♣ 9 7 6 3

♠ K 10 9 8
♥ Q 10 8 3
♦ K J 10
♣ 10 2

♠ A J 7 6 3
♥ A 5
♦ 7 3
♣ A Q J 8

**Suggested
Bidding**

WEST	NORTH	EAST	SOUTH
			1♠
PASS	1NT	PASS	2♣
PASS	2♠	PASS	PASS
PASS			

After South opens 1♠, North, holding three-card support, knows the partnership belongs in spades. However, with only six high-card points and flat distribution, North has a minimal raise and doesn't want to encourage opener to continue bidding with anything less than a maximum opening. Using the forcing 1NT, North has a method to keep the bidding alive and put the partnership in its eight-card fit without promising much in the way of values.

North starts with a forcing 1NT, knowing opener can't pass. After South shows the club suit, North gives a simple preference back to 2♠. This is less encouraging than a direct raise to 2♠. South can't even be sure that responder has three-card support. Responder would still give preference to 2♠ with only two-card support.

South has a medium-strength hand, but the spades are poor and there is no guaranteed eight-card fit. South may decide to settle for a quiet partscore. If South does decide to show some extra strength by bidding 2NT at this point, North will go back to 3♠, and South will definitely be discouraged from bidding any higher.

Suggested Opening Lead

West would likely lead the ♥2, fourth best in one of the unbid suits. West doesn't want to lead a diamond away from the ♦A.

Suggested Play

Declarer has a sure spade, a heart, and four clubs. If the missing spades are divided 3-2, declarer can establish two tricks through length. Declarer's initial plan is to play the ♠A and a low spade, hoping the spades are 3-2.

When West's ♠Q falls under the ♠A, declarer must reconsider. West might have started with the doubleton ♠K-Q, or the ♠Q might be a singleton. To guard against the ♠Q being a singleton, declarer should cross to dummy's ♣K and lead the second round of spades from dummy. If East plays low, declarer plays the ♠J. On the actual deal, the ♠J wins and declarer can then start playing the club winners. East will get two spade tricks to go with a heart trick and two diamond tricks, but that's all.

If West had started with the ♠K-Q, declarer's ♠J would lose to West's ♠K, but now the spades would have divided 3-2, so again declarer would lose only two spades. On the actual deal, if East chooses to play the ♠K when a low spade is led from dummy, declarer eventually gets a trick with the ♠J.

Suggested Defense

The defenders will get only two spades, a heart, and two diamonds if declarer plays the spade suit correctly. They can get a third spade trick if declarer plays the ♠A and then a low spade from the South hand. If North-South get higher than 2♠, they can be defeated.

Conclusion

In standard bidding, the partnership is almost certain to get too high:

WEST	NORTH	EAST	SOUTH
			1♠
PASS	2♠	PASS	3♣/3♠/4♠?

After North raises immediately to 2♠, South can hardly do less than make a game try of 3♣ or 3♠. Some players might even take their chances with an immediate jump to 4♠.

Using the forcing 1NT, the partnership has a chance to stop in 2♠ and, at worst, stop in 3♠.

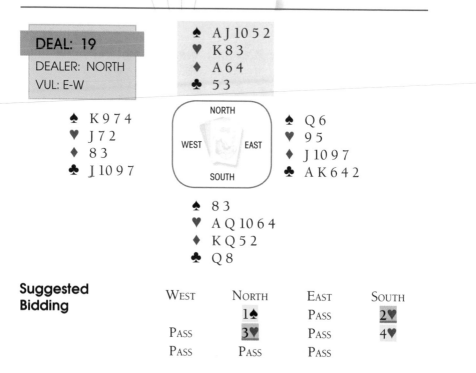

		♠ AJ1052	
DEAL: 19		♥ K83	
DEALER: NORTH		♦ A64	
VUL: E-W		♣ 53	

West:
♠ K974
♥ J72
♦ 83
♣ J1097

East:
♠ Q6
♥ 95
♦ J1097
♣ AK642

South:
♠ 83
♥ AQ1064
♦ KQ52
♣ Q8

Suggested Bidding

WEST	NORTH	EAST	SOUTH
	1♠	PASS	2♥
PASS	3♥	PASS	4♥
PASS	PASS	PASS	

Over North's 1♠ opening, South makes a 2/1 game-forcing response of 2♥. Since the 2♥ response promises a five-card or longer heat suit, North can raise to 3♥ with three-card support, agreeing on hearts as the trump suit[40].

With a minimum for the 2/1 response, South has no interest in slam. So South simply continues to game in 4♥. North also has nothing extra, and the partnership stops comfortably in a game contract.

Suggested Opening Lead

West would lead the ♣J, top of the solid sequence in one of the unbid suits.

---

[40] North might use the principle of fast arrival and jump to 4♥, but with two aces and a valuable ♥K, slam is possible if responder is interested.

Suggested Play

If the missing hearts are favorably divided, declarer has five heart tricks to go with the ♠A and three diamond winners. That's nine tricks. If the missing diamonds are divided 3-3, declarer can get a tenth trick that way, but that's against the odds.

The spade suit offers a 75% chance of providing a tenth trick. Suppose East wins the first two club tricks and switches to the ♦J. Declarer wins the ♦Q, and draws trumps with the ♥A, ♥K, and back to the ♥Q when the hearts divide 3-2[41]. Then declarer leads a low spade and plays dummy's ♠10 when West follows with a low spade. This loses to East's ♠Q. Suppose East returns a club, since there are no trumps left in dummy. Declarer ruffs, and plays a low diamond to the ♦A and a diamond back to the ♦K. If the diamonds had divided 3-3, declarer has the rest of the tricks. When it turns out that the diamonds are divided 4-2, declarer leads the remaining low spade and finesses dummy's ♠J. This wins, and declarer can discard the losing diamond on dummy's ♠A.

The repeated finesse in spades will work if West has the ♠K, ♠Q, or ♠K and ♠Q. It loses only if East holds both the ♠K and ♠Q. That's a 75% chance of success. Since declarer also has the opportunity to discover whether the missing diamonds are divided 3-3 before trying the second spade finesse, declarer's overall chance for success is over 80%, much better than the 35% chance of diamonds dividing 3-3.

Suggested Defense

After winning the ♣A-K, East shouldn't lead a third round of clubs. That would allow declarer to discard either a spade or diamond loser and ruff in dummy. A diamond switch is safest. If declarer doesn't play on spades, East can hold on to the diamonds to defeat the contract with two clubs, a diamond, and a spade trick.

Conclusion

A response of 2♥ over an opening bid of 1♠ promises a five-card or longer suit. With three or more hearts, opener can agree on hearts as trumps.

---

[41] Playing hearts this way, declarer would be in a position to finesse the ♥10 on the third round if hearts were divided 4-1 with East holding four hearts including the ♥J.

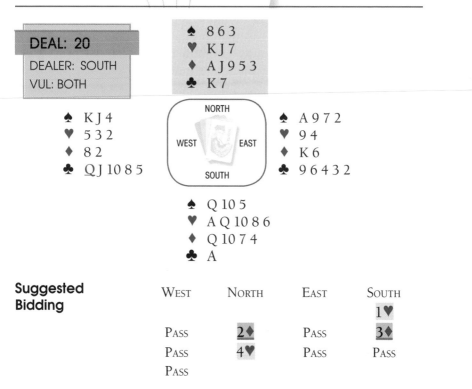

DEAL: 20	♠ 863
	♥ K J 7
DEALER: SOUTH	♦ A J 9 5 3
VUL: BOTH	♣ K 7

NORTH

♠ K J 4   WEST   EAST   ♠ A 9 7 2
♥ 5 3 2   ♥ 9 4
♦ 8 2   ♦ K 6
♣ Q J 10 8 5   SOUTH   ♣ 9 6 4 3 2

♠ Q 10 5
♥ A Q 10 8 6
♦ Q 10 7 4
♣ A

Suggested Bidding

WEST	NORTH	EAST	SOUTH
			1♥
PASS	2♦	PASS	3♦[42]
PASS	4♥	PASS	PASS
PASS			

South opens 1♥. With three-card support and 12 high-card points plus 1 dummy point for the doubleton club, North starts with a new suit, 2♦. With four-card support for diamonds, South raises to 3♦[42].

North always intended to play with hearts as the trump suit. Following the principle of fast arrival, North jumps to 4♥, showing no interest in slam. A raise to only 3♥ would tend to show extra values and slam interest. South has some extra values, but with North showing no interest in slam, settles for game.

Suggested Opening Lead

With little help from the auction, West is likely to lead the ♣Q, top of the solid sequence. This appears safer than leading a spade away from the ♠K-J.

---

[42] South could make a *splinter bid* of 4♣, but most players avoid this bid when holding a singleton ace. If South does bid 4♣, North will put the partnership back in 4♥.

Suggested Play

Declarer starts with five hearts, a diamond, and two clubs. Declarer could develop four more diamond tricks with the help of a finesse if West holds the ♦K. Even if the diamond finesse loses, as on the actual layout, declarer has enough diamond tricks to make the contract.

There is a danger. The defenders may be able to take four tricks before declarer has the extra diamond winners established. If West leads a low spade at trick one, the defenders can take the first three spade tricks. When the diamond finesse loses, the defenders will have four tricks. Down one.

On a club lead, however, declarer can make the contract even if the diamond finesse loses. After winning the ♣A, declarer can cross to dummy with a heart and discard a spade on the ♣K. After drawing trumps, declarer can then safely take the diamond finesse. When it loses, the defenders can take two spade tricks, but that's all.

Suggested Defense

A lead of the ♠4 will defeat the contract. East wins the ♠A and returns a spade. The defenders get three spade tricks and can wait around to get a trick with East's ♦K. Down one. However, West's natural lead is the ♣Q. West is only likely to find a spade lead if the North-South auction, through control-showing bids, pinpoints that a spade is the best lead.

Conclusion

If North raises to only 3♥ on the second round, South will likely show slam interest with a control-showing bid of 4♣. Even if North-South stop in 4♥, West might be tipped off to lead a spade rather than a club.

The principle of fast arrival serves a dual purpose. It warns partner not to go looking for a slam with only marginal interest, and it avoids giving the opponents information which might help them find the best defense.

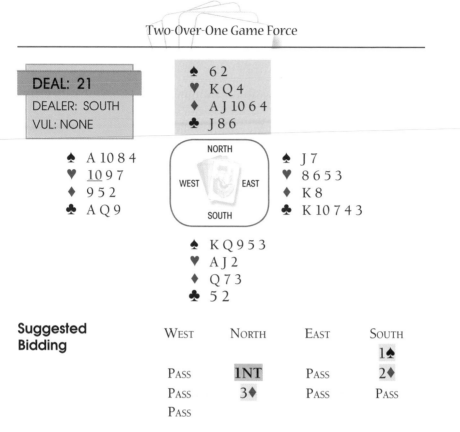

DEAL: 21

DEALER: SOUTH
VUL: NONE

North
♠ 6 2
♥ K Q 4
♦ A J 10 6 4
♣ J 8 6

West
♠ A 10 8 4
♥ 10 9 7
♦ 9 5 2
♣ A Q 9

East
♠ J 7
♥ 8 6 5 3
♦ K 8
♣ K 10 7 4 3

South
♠ K Q 9 5 3
♥ A J 2
♦ Q 7 3
♣ 5 2

Suggested Bidding

WEST	NORTH	EAST	SOUTH
			1♠
PASS	1NT	PASS	2♦
PASS	3♦	PASS	PASS
PASS			

South opens 1♠ and West passes. North has 11 high-card points plus 1 length point for the five-card diamond suit. That's not quite enough for a game-forcing 2/1 response. So North starts with a forcing 1NT.

In standard methods, South could pass the 1NT response with a minimum balanced hand. Since 1NT is forcing, however, South has to find another bid. South bids 2♦, a three-card minor. With 12 points, North wants to invite game, and with five-card support for diamonds, raises to 3♦.

South doesn't really want to play with diamonds as the trump suit, but with a minimum hand, the only way to reject the invitation is by passing. If South bids again, the partnership will get to game, which is likely to be too high. South has to trust that North is aware that 2♦ could be bid on a three-card suit. With a minimum, opener passes and hopes for the best.

Suggested Opening Lead

West will probably lead the ♥10, top of the broken sequence in an unbid suit.

Suggested Play

Declarer has three sure heart winners and a diamond. Three more diamond tricks will be promoted once the ♦K is driven out, and declarer may be able to take all the diamond tricks with the help of a finesse if West holds the ♦K. Declarer can also promote a spade winner, and might get two spade tricks by leading toward the ♠Q and ♠K if East has the ♠A.

A reasonable approach is to plan on ruffing a club in the South hand. Even though South is declarer, it is declarer's hand that has the short trumps. Declarer wins the first heart trick and leads a club, giving a trick to the opponents. If the defenders lead another heart[43], declarer can give up a second club trick. On regaining the lead, declarer will be able to ruff a club in the South hand. This guarantees five diamond tricks, even if the diamond finesse loses. Together with three hearts and a spade, declarer has nine tricks.

By not drawing trumps right away, declarer runs some risk that the defenders may get a heart ruff if the missing hearts are divided 5-2 or 6-1 rather than 4-3. If that's the case, declarer can still fall back on the diamond finesse. Declarer can usually judge from defenders' signals whether a heart ruff is likely. On this deal, East will likely make a discouraging signal in hearts.

Suggested Defense

If declarer does win the first trick with the ♥A and takes the diamond finesse, the defenders can defeat the contract by continuing to lead diamonds to prevent declarer from ruffing a club. This is a challenging defense to find.

Conclusion

After a forcing 1NT response, declarer may have to bid a three-card minor suit when holding a minimum balanced hand. Opener doesn't plan to play in the minor suit, but may have to if responder raises and opener doesn't have enough to bid again. Opener shouldn't worry about declaring with a three-card trump suit. It may be the best contract for the partnership.

---

[43] If the defenders lead trumps, declarer can switch plans and go about establishing an extra spade winner through length.

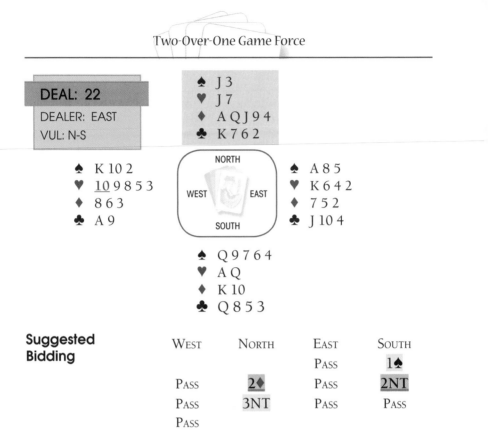

DEAL: 22

DEALER: EAST
VUL: N-S

♠ J 3
♥ J 7
♦ A Q J 9 4
♣ K 7 6 2

♠ K 10 2
♥ 10 9 8 5 3
♦ 8 6 3
♣ A 9

NORTH

WEST   EAST

SOUTH

♠ A 8 5
♥ K 6 4 2
♦ 7 5 2
♣ J 10 4

♠ Q 9 7 6 4
♥ A Q
♦ K 10
♣ Q 8 5 3

Suggested Bidding

WEST	NORTH	EAST	SOUTH
		PASS	1♠
PASS	2♦	PASS	2NT
PASS	3NT	PASS	PASS
PASS			

South opens 1♠ and North makes a 2/1 game-forcing response of 2♦. Opener now has to choose a rebid. To show the second suit, opener would have to bid 3♣. To bid a new suit at the three level, opener should have either extra strength, about 15 or more points, or extra distribution, a five-card or longer suit. Here opener has neither. With a minimum semi-balanced hand, the most descriptive rebid opener can make is 2NT.

Responder has a similar decision. Over the 2NT rebid, North could show the club suit by bidding 3♣. However, once South hasn't shown a club suit, it's unlikely that the partnership belongs in clubs. So North simply raises to 3NT, the most likely game contract.

Suggested Opening Lead

Against 3NT, West would lead the ♥10, top of the solid sequence in West's longest suit.

Suggested Play

The opening heart lead guarantees two heart winners to go with the five diamond tricks. Declarer needs two more. There won't be time to develop tricks in spades. The lead would have to be given up at least twice, and by then, the defenders will have established enough heart winners to defeat the contract. So declarer will have to get two tricks from the club suit without giving up the lead twice.

To get two club tricks without giving up the lead twice, declarer needs one defender to hold a singleton or doubleton ♣A. After winning the first heart, declarer can lead a low club toward dummy. If West plays the ♣A, declarer has an easy time getting tricks with both the ♣K and ♣Q. So West will likely play low, letting declarer win dummy's ♣K. Declarer now leads another club, and when East plays the ♣10 or ♣J, declarer knows it won't do any good to play the ♣Q since West holds the ♣A. Instead, declarer plays a low club, hoping West's ♣A is now singleton. That works on the actual layout, and declarer gets three club tricks, finishing with an overtrick!

Why play West to have a singleton or doubleton ♣A rather than East? Having won the first trick in the South hand, it's easier to play West to be the defender who has a singleton or doubleton ♣A. Also, since West chose to lead a heart, declarer can infer that West likely has more hearts than East, and therefore fewer clubs. There's no guarantee, and declarer might choose to cross to dummy with a diamond to start clubs by leading toward the ♣Q. Unfortunately, this doesn't work on the actual deal. The ♣Q is taken by the ♣A, and declarer loses two clubs.

Suggested Defense

If declarer doesn't find the winning play in clubs, the defenders can establish three hearts to go with the ♠A-K and ♣A to defeat 3NT.

Conclusion

If South chooses to show clubs, the partnership may get too high.

West	North	East	South
			1♠
Pass	2♦	Pass	3♣
Pass	4♣	Pass	?

North will likely raise clubs, expecting South to have extra strength or distribution. Once the partnership gets beyond 3NT, it is too high.

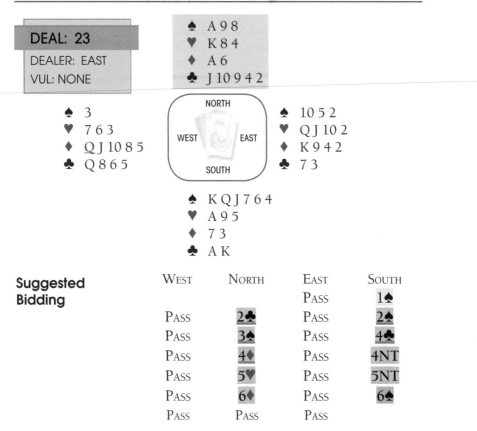

	WEST	NORTH	EAST	SOUTH
Suggested Bidding			PASS	1♠
	PASS	2♣	PASS	2♠
	PASS	3♠	PASS	4♣
	PASS	4♦	PASS	4NT
	PASS	5♥	PASS	5NT
	PASS	6♦	PASS	6♠
	PASS	PASS	PASS	

After South opens 1♠ and North responds 2♣, South doesn't need to jump to show the extra strength. South can simply rebid 2♠, since that is still forcing. Once North raises to show the spade fit, South has enough strength that slam is likely[44]. However, South shouldn't use Blackwood with two low diamonds. If North were to show only one ace, South still wouldn't know whether the defenders can take the first two diamond tricks.

So South makes a control-showing bid of 4♣. North cooperates by showing the ♦A. Now it is safe for South to use Blackwood. Once North shows two aces, South might consider a grand slam and ask about kings. When North shows only one, South will settle for a small slam.

Suggested Opening Lead

West will lead the ♦Q against the slam, top of the solid sequence.

---

[44] If North uses the principle of fast arrival and jumps to 4♠, South has enough strength to continue bidding to slam anyway. South could make a control-showing bid of 5♣.

Suggested Play

Declarer has six sure spades, two hearts, a diamond, and two clubs. That's eleven tricks. Declarer needs one more, and it will have to come from clubs.

After winning the ♦A, declarer can draw two rounds of trumps with the ♠K and ♠Q, leaving the ♠A as an entry to dummy. Then declarer can take the ♣A-K, before leading to dummy's ♠A to draw East's remaining trump. Now declarer leads dummy's ♣J. When East shows out, declarer discards the ♦7 on the ♣J, losing the trick to West's ♣Q. This is referred to as discarding a *loser on a loser*. The losing diamond is discarded on a trick that is lost to the opponent's ♣Q.

Although declarer loses this trick, dummy's remaining clubs are now established as winners. If West leads a diamond after winning the ♣Q, declarer ruffs. Declarer then crosses to dummy with the ♥K and discards a heart on dummy's established ♣10. Declarer has the rest of the tricks.

Suggested Defense

Declarer can make the slam by establishing the clubs. If declarer doesn't do this, the defenders will eventually get a diamond trick and a heart trick to defeat the contract.

Conclusion

If South used Blackwood on this deal after North raises spades, there would be no problem reaching slam since North has two aces. However, North might have held either of these hands:

1.		2.	
♠	A 9 8	♠	10 9 8
♥	K Q 4	♥	K 8 4
♦	J 6	♦	A K
♣	Q J 10 4 2	♣	Q J 10 4 2

North would have shown one ace with either hand, and South would not know whether to bid a slam. Opposite the first hand, slam is not a good contract since the defenders can take the first two diamond tricks. Opposite the second hand, slam is an excellent spot since the only trick declarer has to lose is the ♠A.

Holding two or more cards in an unbid suit with no ace or king, start with a control-showing bid rather than Blackwood.

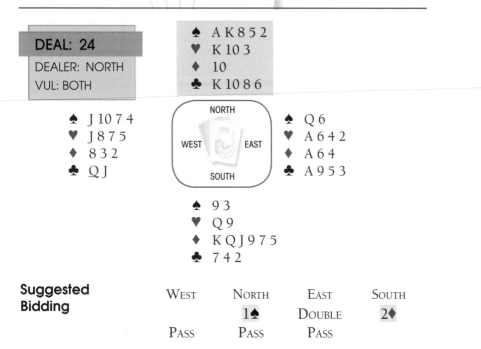

	DEAL: 24	♠ A K 8 5 2
		♥ K 10 3
	DEALER: NORTH	♦ 10
	VUL: BOTH	♣ K 10 8 6

NORTH

♠ J 10 7 4
♥ J 8 7 5
♦ 8 3 2
♣ Q J

WEST   EAST

SOUTH

♠ Q 6
♥ A 6 4 2
♦ A 6 4
♣ A 9 5 3

♠ 9 3
♥ Q 9
♦ K Q J 9 7 5
♣ 7 4 2

Suggested Bidding

WEST	NORTH	EAST	SOUTH
	1♠	DOUBLE	2♦
PASS	PASS	PASS	

Over North's 1♠ opening bid, East makes a takeout double, holding 14 high-card points and support for the unbid suits.

Once responder's right-hand opponent overcalls or doubles, 2/1 Game Force no longer applies. The partnership reverts to standard methods. Responder can start with a redouble holding 10 or more high-card points. A consequence of this is that a new suit response at the two level is not forcing after a takeout double. So South can bid 2♦ with this hand, to show a good diamond suit and fewer than 10 high-card points.

West doesn't have enough to compete at the two level and passes. With a minimum opening and no fit for partner's suit, North should simply pass the 2♦ response. Bidding any more is likely to get the partnership too high. East has nothing more to say, and South becomes declarer in 2♦.

Suggested Opening Lead

West would likely lead the ♣Q, top of the touching cards.

Suggested Play

Declarer has two sure spade tricks and can promote a trick in hearts and five tricks in diamonds. That's enough to make the contract.

When West leads the ♣Q, declarer can be fairly certain that East holds the ♣A. Declarer can try to turn dummy's ♣10 into a winner by covering with the ♣K. However, the defenders can prevent declarer from winning a club trick by trumping the third round before declarer can draw trumps.

Suggested Defense

If West leads the ♣Q and declarer covers with the ♣K, East can win the ♣A and return a club to West's ♣J. When East wins a trick with the ♥A or ♦A, East can lead another club and West can ruff. That holds declarer to eight tricks.

Conclusion

Even when the partnership is playing 2/1 Game Force, it won't come up on most auctions. The partnership still needs to know how to handle other 'standard' auctions. When the opponents interfere, many agreements change from non-competitive auctions, as other bids such as doubles and cuebids come into play.

2/1 Game Force doesn't apply when responder's right-hand opponent overcalls or doubles.

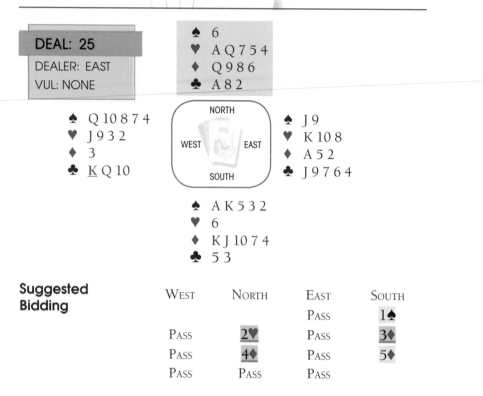

DEAL: 25

DEALER: EAST
VUL: NONE

♠ 6
♥ A Q 7 5 4
♦ Q 9 8 6
♣ A 8 2

NORTH

WEST   EAST

SOUTH

♠ Q 10 8 7 4
♥ J 9 3 2
♦ 3
♣ K Q 10

♠ J 9
♥ K 10 8
♦ A 5 2
♣ J 9 7 6 4

♠ A K 5 3 2
♥ 6
♦ K J 10 7 4
♣ 5 3

Suggested Bidding

WEST	NORTH	EAST	SOUTH
		PASS	1♠
PASS	2♥	PASS	3♦
PASS	4♦	PASS	5♦
PASS	PASS	PASS	

With two five-card suits, South opens the higher-ranking, 1♠. With 12 high-card points plus 1 length point for the five-card suit, North has enough to make a 2/1 game-forcing response of 2♥, showing the five-card suit.

To show the second suit, South has to go to the three level, using up some of the bidding room. That's okay if South has either extra strength or extra distribution. Here South has a minimum opening bid, but the 5-5 distribution is enough to bid the second suit at the three level. With four-card support, North raises. North can afford to go past 3NT with the knowledge that South has extra values either in high-cards or shape.

With a minimum, South simply continues to game in 5♦. North also doesn't have enough extra to bid again, so the partnership settles for game.

Suggested Opening Lead

West would lead the ♣K, top of the broken sequence in the unbid suit.

Suggested Play

Declarer has only four top tricks, the ♠A-K, ♥A, and ♣A. Seven more tricks are needed. Four tricks can be promoted in diamonds, and there are various additional possibilities such as the heart finesse, establishing the spade suit through length, and ruffing spades in dummy.

On a deal like this, with shortness in both hands and a lot of trumps, declarer should consider a *crossruff*. The good trump spots make this a good possibility, since the only key missing high trump is the ♦A. If the defenders overruff, it will have to be with the ♦A, and that's a trick declarer has to lose anyway. When planning a crossruff, declarer should count the tricks likely to be available, to see if that will be enough. Declarer can plan to get at least seven tricks from the trump suit by ruffing spades in the dummy and hearts in declarer's hand. Declarer should also plan to take the winners in other suits early, so the defenders can't discard their low cards in those suits and perhaps ruff one of declarer's winners near the end of the hand

So declarer wins the ♣A, plays the ♥A and ruffs a heart. It's relatively safe to ruff this trick with the ♦4, since it will only be overruffed if the missing hearts are divided 6-1. Now declarer takes the ♠A-K, and ruffs a spade. East can overruff with the ♦A and lead a trump to remove one of dummy's trumps, but that's okay. Declarer can continue ruffing hearts and spades, and will finish with eleven tricks.

Suggested Defense

The ♣K would be a popular lead from the West hand, but holding a lot of cards in declarer's first bid suit, spades, West might also consider leading a trump, visualizing that declarer is likely going to trump spade losers in the dummy. Declarer can still make the contract[45], but it would be a good try.

Conclusion

North and South do well to reach 5♦ on this deal. A contract of 3NT will be defeated if the defenders lead clubs. Opener's rebid of a new suit at the three level shows extra distribution – a five-card suit – or extra strength – about 15 or more high-card points.

---

[45] Declarer can ruff a couple of hearts to establish dummy's suit when East's ♥K falls. Declarer can actually make an overtrick if the defenders start with two rounds of diamonds.

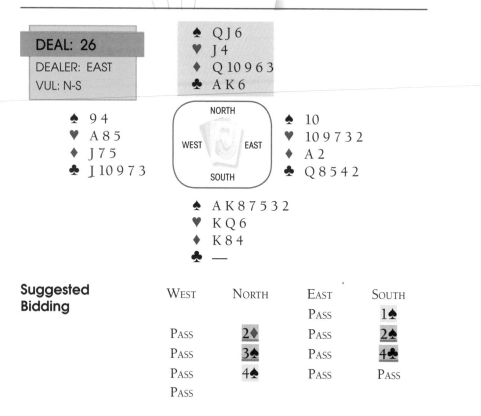

	WEST	NORTH	EAST	SOUTH
Suggested Bidding			PASS	1♠
	PASS	2♦	PASS	2♠
	PASS	3♠	PASS	4♣
	PASS	4♠	PASS	PASS
	PASS			

South opens with 1♠. North has 13 high-card points and three-card support for spades. North plans to take the partnership to game in spades but starts with a 2/1 response of 2♦. Since the partnership is already committed to game, South doesn't need to jump and can simply rebid 2♠. Now North can show the spade support with a raise to 3♠.

South has enough to consider slam, but Blackwood shouldn't be used with a void. If North shows one ace, as on the actual deal, South won't know if it's the ♥A, ♦A, or the ♣A—which won't be of much use. So South makes a control-showing bid of 4♣. Looking at the ♣A-K, North may be a little surprised that South shows a control in clubs, but can visualize that it is probably a club void. With no control to show in either diamonds or hearts, North returns to the agreed trump suit, 4♠. Since North has not shown first-round control in either diamonds or hearts, South has to settle for game, knowing two key aces are missing.

Suggested Opening Lead

West would likely choose the ♣J, top of the solid sequence. Even though South bid clubs, it showed a control, not a suit, so leading a club is reasonable. The alternative of leading a heart when holding the ♥A, or one of the opponents' suits is not particularly attractive.

Suggested Play

There's nothing to the play. Declarer has eleven tricks and no more. The defenders will get the ♥A and ♦A.

Suggested Defense

Even after West leads a club, declarer can't avoid losing tricks. Declarer can discard two red cards on the ♣A-K, but must still give the defenders their two aces.

Conclusion

If South bid Blackwood on this deal, North would show one ace. If South assumed it was likely to be the ♥A or ♦A, the partnership would then get to a slam that can't be made. Of course, North might have held either of these hands, which would make slam an excellent contract:

1.	♠ Q J 6	2.	♠ Q J 6
	♥ J 4		♥ A 4
	♦ A Q 10 9 6		♦ Q J 9 6 3
	♣ K 6 3		♣ K 6 3

When South makes a control-showing bid of 4♣, North would cooperate by bidding 4♦ with the first hand or 4♥ with the second. In both cases, South could now confidently bid to 6♠.

When holding a void, it is rarely useful to use the Blackwood convention to ask for aces. The responses to Blackwood show only the number of aces and kings, not specific aces and kings.

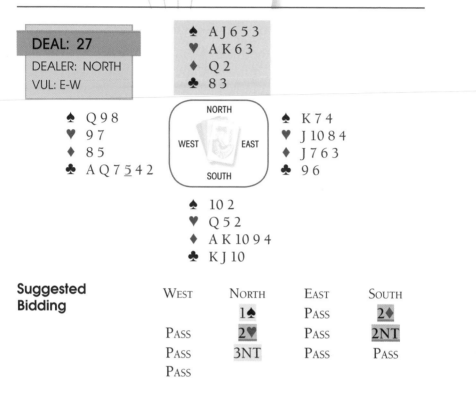

DEAL: 27

DEALER: NORTH
VUL: E-W

NORTH
♠ A J 6 5 3
♥ A K 6 3
♦ Q 2
♣ 8 3

WEST
♠ Q 9 8
♥ 9 7
♦ 8 5
♣ A Q 7 5 4 2

EAST
♠ K 7 4
♥ J 10 8 4
♦ J 7 6 3
♣ 9 6

SOUTH
♠ 10 2
♥ Q 5 2
♦ A K 10 9 4
♣ K J 10

Suggested Bidding

WEST	NORTH	EAST	SOUTH
	1♠	PASS	2♦
PASS	2♥	PASS	2NT
PASS	3NT	PASS	PASS
PASS			

North opens 1♠. South, with 13 high-card points plus 1 length point for the fifth diamond, has enough for a game-forcing 2♦ response.

North now shows the second suit by bidding 2♥. South can't raise opener's second suit with only three-card support. Instead, South suggests playing in notrump by bidding 2NT. There's no need to jump to 3NT. The 2NT rebid is forcing and leaves room for North to further describe the hand.

North, having already shown the spades and hearts, is content to raise to game in notrump. South has nothing more to say.

Suggested Opening Lead

West would likely lead the ♣5, fourth highest from the long suit.

Suggested Play

Declarer will win the first club trick when East plays the ♣9. Declarer also has a sure trick in spades, three in hearts, and three in diamonds. So one more trick is needed.

Declarer might get an extra trick from the heart suit if the six missing hearts are divided 3-3, but that's against the odds. The diamond suit is much better. It offers 100% chance to get an extra trick, and it might provide two extra tricks if the missing diamonds are divided 3-3, or if the ♦J falls singleton or doubleton. However, there is a danger. From the opening lead and play to the first trick, it appears that West has the ♣A-Q. If East gains the lead while developing an extra trick in diamonds, East can lead a club, and the defenders will take enough club tricks to defeat the contract. East is the dangerous opponent. It won't matter if a diamond trick is lost to West, since West can't lead that club without giving South a trick with the ♣K. West is the safe opponent.

After winning the first club trick, declarer should play a diamond to dummy's ♦Q and then lead a low diamond and finesse the ♦10, or ♦9. On the actual deal, the finesse wins, and declarer will finish with an overtrick. If West held the ♦J, the finesse would lose, but the contract would be safe. The safe opponent would be on lead, and declarer's remaining diamonds would be winners.

Suggested Defense

If declarer simply takes the top three diamonds and then gives up a trick to East's ♦J, a club return from East will defeat the contract two tricks.

Conclusion

In standard bidding, the partnership would get to the same contract:

West	North	East	South
	1♠	Pass	2♦
Pass	2♥	Pass	3NT
Pass	Pass	Pass	

South would have to jump to 3NT on the second round, since a rebid of 2NT would not be forcing. That works fine on the actual deal, but would lead to an uncomfortable dilemma for North if North held six spades or five hearts. North wouldn't know whether or not to bid again over the jump to 3NT.

Using 2/1 Game Force, the partnership can go slowly, giving each partner an opportunity to describe the hand and then settle on the best contract.

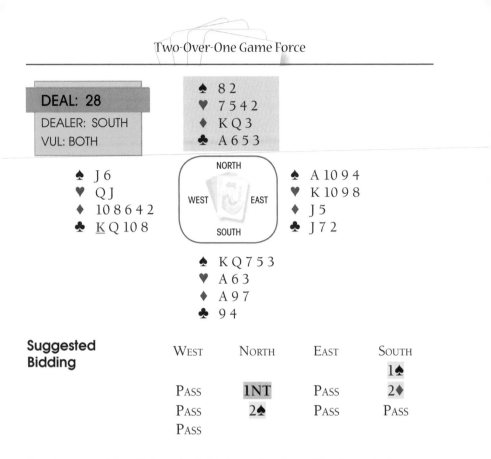

DEAL: 28

DEALER: SOUTH
VUL: BOTH

NORTH

♠ 8 2
♥ 7 5 4 2
♦ K Q 3
♣ A 6 5 3

WEST

♠ J 6
♥ Q J
♦ 10 8 6 4 2
♣ K Q 10 8

EAST

♠ A 10 9 4
♥ K 10 9 8
♦ J 5
♣ J 7 2

SOUTH

♠ K Q 7 5 3
♥ A 6 3
♦ A 9 7
♣ 9 4

Suggested Bidding

WEST	NORTH	EAST	SOUTH
			1♠
PASS	1NT	PASS	2♦
PASS	2♠	PASS	PASS
PASS			

South opens 1♠. With only 9 high-card points, North can't do more than respond 1NT. Playing 2/1, the 1NT response is forcing, so South must find a rebid with the minimum balanced hand. South bids 2♦, the longer minor.

North actually prefers diamonds to spades, but should not pass the 2♦ rebid with this hand. There are two reasons. South could have only a three-card diamond suit, as on the actual deal. Also, South could have a medium-strength hand of about 17–18 points, not quite enough for a jump shift. So North should bid 2♠, putting the partnership back into the known seven-card fit. This is technically referred to as false preference.

With a minimum opening bid, South accepts North's preference back to 2♠ and passes.

Suggested Opening Lead

West would lead the ♣K against 2♠, top of the broken sequence.

Suggested Play

Declarer starts with a heart trick, three diamonds, and a club, for a total of five. Three more tricks are needed, and they will need to come from the spade suit.

Declarer should plan to take a repeated finesse in spades by leading spades twice from the dummy, hoping East has the ♠A. After winning the ♣A, declarer leads a low spade. If East plays low, declarer wins the trick with the ♠Q. Declarer then goes back to dummy with a diamond and leads another spade. If East plays low, declarer wins the ♠K. If East plays the ♠A, declarer's ♠K will win a trick later.

Playing this way, East will get only two spade tricks and declarer will get three, even though the missing spades are divided 4-2. That's just enough to make 2♠.

Suggested Defense

The defenders can establish a club trick and two heart tricks. If declarer leads the ♠K or ♠Q instead of leading toward the honors, East can win the ♠A and will get three spade tricks to defeat the contract.

Conclusion

In standard methods, South would pass North's 1NT response. That's a reasonable contract, since North can get two spade winners with the help of the repeated finesse, to go with the three diamond tricks and the ♥A and ♣A. That's seven tricks. The defenders can develop six winners before declarer can develop a third spade trick. In a spade contract, declarer can take eight tricks.

Using the forcing 1NT, responder needs to be aware that opener's rebid may be a three-card minor suit. The partnership can't stop in 1NT, but will often reach an equally good or better contract than when using standard methods.

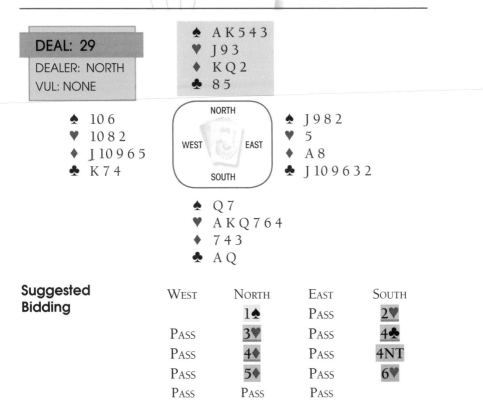

DEAL: 29

DEALER: NORTH
VUL: NONE

♠ A K 5 4 3
♥ J 9 3
♦ K Q 2
♣ 8 5

NORTH

WEST   EAST

SOUTH

♠ 10 6
♥ 10 8 2
♦ J 10 9 6 5
♣ K 7 4

♠ J 9 8 2
♥ 5
♦ A 8
♣ J 10 9 6 3 2

♠ Q 7
♥ A K Q 7 6 4
♦ 7 4 3
♣ A Q

Suggested Bidding

WEST	NORTH	EAST	SOUTH
	1♠	PASS	2♥
PASS	3♥	PASS	4♣
PASS	4♦	PASS	4NT
PASS	5♦	PASS	6♥
PASS	PASS	PASS	

North opens 1♠ and South makes a 2/1 response of 2♥. Since South has promised a five-card or longer heart suit, North can raise to 3♥ with three-card support.

Now that the partnership has agreed upon a trump suit, South is interested in reaching a slam. With no control in the unbid diamond suit, South can't bid Blackwood right away. So South starts a control-showing sequence by bidding 4♣ to show the club control. North has nothing extra and doesn't want to take the partnership past the game level of 4♥ to show the first-round control in spades. However, North can cooperate below the game level by bidding 4♦ to show the second-round control in diamonds.

South is no longer concerned about the diamond suit, and can assume the captaincy and bid Blackwood. When North shows one ace, South knows there is only one ace missing, and can put the partnership in 6♥.

Suggested Opening Lead

Although North bid diamonds, it was a control-showing bid, not a suit. So West might choose the ♦J, top of the solid sequence.

Suggested Play

Declarer has three sure spade tricks, six sure heart tricks, and the ♣A. When the defenders lead diamonds, dummy's ♦K-Q is promoted into a winner. So declarer needs one more trick.

The club suit offers a 50% chance of success, but the spade suit offers nearly 85% chance of developing an extra trick. Declarer can establish at least one extra spade trick if the suit is divided either 3-3 or 4-2. Only if the missing spades are divided 5-1 or 6-0 will declarer be unable to use the spade suit.

Suppose East wins the first trick with the ♦A and then leads a club. Declarer can win the ♣A and draw the defenders' trumps. Then declarer takes the ♠Q and plays the ♠7 to dummy's ♠K. When both defenders follow suit, the contract is assured. Declarer plays the ♠A and discards the diamond loser or the ♣Q. When the missing spades prove to be divided 4-2, declarer leads another spade and trumps it. That makes dummy's last spade a winner. Declarer crosses to dummy's diamond winner and discards the remaining loser on the last spade. That's twelve tricks.

Suggested Defense

The 6♥ contract can't be defeated if declarer establishes the spade suit. The best lead is a diamond, since a club lead would give declarer a twelfth trick right away.

Conclusion

Once the trump suit has been established and one partner starts a control-showing sequence, the other partner can cooperate below the game level whenever possible, even with a minimum hand. Either a first- or second-round control can be shown. Blackwood can subsequently be used to make sure the partnership isn't missing two aces.

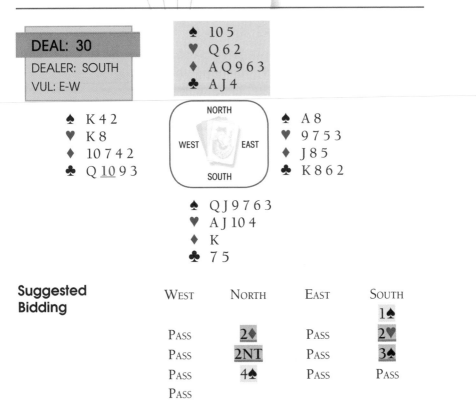

DEAL: 30

DEALER: SOUTH

VUL: E-W

♠ 10 5
♥ Q 6 2
♦ A Q 9 6 3
♣ A J 4

NORTH

WEST   EAST

SOUTH

♠ K 4 2
♥ K 8
♦ 10 7 4 2
♣ Q 10 9 3

♠ A 8
♥ 9 7 5 3
♦ J 8 5
♣ K 8 6 2

♠ Q J 9 7 6 3
♥ A J 10 4
♦ K
♣ 7 5

Suggested Bidding

WEST	NORTH	EAST	SOUTH
			1♠
PASS	2♦	PASS	2♥
PASS	2NT	PASS	3♠
PASS	4♠	PASS	PASS
PASS			

With 11 high-card points plus 2 length points for the six-card spade suit, South has enough to open the bidding 1♠. North responds 2♦ and South shows the second suit by bidding 2♥. South shouldn't bypass a four-card heart suit to rebid the six-card spade suit. North could have a four-card heart suit and not be able to bid it over 1♠ since a 2♥ response would show five or more hearts.

Over South's 2♥ rebid, North doesn't have to jump to game. Instead, North can rebid 2NT, suggesting notrump as a contract and also giving opener an opportunity to further describe the hand. South rebids the six-card spade suit to finish describing the distribution. Now North knows the partnership has an eight-card spade fit and can put the partnership in a game contract of 4♠.

Suggested Opening Lead

West can lead the ♣10, top of the touching cards from an interior sequence in the unbid suit.

Suggested Play

Declarer has the ♥A and ♣A, as well as three potential diamond winners. Taking the diamonds may be challenging since the suit is blocked. Once the ♣A is gone, dummy has no sure entry. Declarer can take the ♦K, but will need to find an entry to dummy to reach the ♦A-Q. Declarer can promote four spades by driving out the ♠A-K and two hearts by driving out the ♥K. Declarer might even be able to take four hearts with the help of a finesse if East holds the ♥K. That's more than enough.

There's a potential problem, however, if declarer leads a spade after winning the ♣A. The defenders will win and take a club trick. Declarer still has to lose another spade trick and may still have to lose a trick to the ♥K. That gives the defenders four tricks. To avoid this, declarer should win the ♣A and immediately play the ♦A, even though declarer's ♦K will fall under it! Declarer can then play dummy's ♦Q and discard a club.

Now it's safe to lead a spade. The defenders can win and lead a club, but declarer ruffs and leads another spade to drive out the remaining high spade. On regaining the lead, declarer draws the last trump and can give up a trick to the ♥K. Declarer loses only two spades and a heart.

Suggested Defense

If declarer doesn't discard a club before leading trumps, the defenders can take their club winner and defeat 4♠ with two spades, and a club. If declarer tries the heart finesse before drawing trumps. West can win the ♥K and lead another heart. On winning the ♠A, East can lead a heart for West to ruff.

Conclusion

In standard bidding, the partnership might miss the eight-card spade fit:

West	North	East	South
			1♠
Pass	2♦	Pass	2♥
Pass	3NT	Pass	Pass?
Pass			

North can't rebid only 2NT, since it's not forcing. If North jumps to 3NT, South won't know whether to bid 4♠ or pass. 3NT can be defeated.

Using 2/1 Game Force, the partnership can explore slowly for the best game contract.

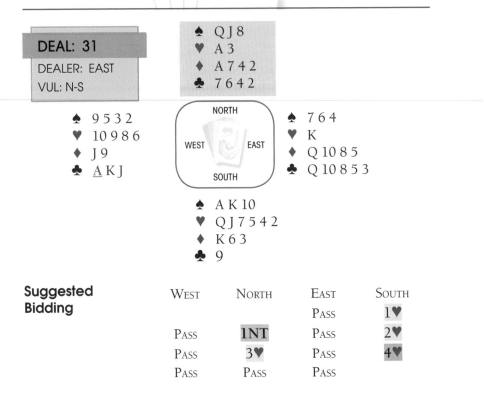

DEAL: 31

DEALER: EAST

VUL: N-S

NORTH

♠ Q J 8
♥ A 3
♦ A 7 4 2
♣ 7 6 4 2

WEST

♠ 9 5 3 2
♥ 10 9 8 6
♦ J 9
♣ A K J

EAST

♠ 7 6 4
♥ K
♦ Q 10 8 5
♣ Q 10 8 5 3

SOUTH

♠ A K 10
♥ Q J 7 5 4 2
♦ K 6 3
♣ 9

Suggested Bidding

WEST	NORTH	EAST	SOUTH
		PASS	1♥
PASS	1NT	PASS	2♥
PASS	3♥	PASS	4♥
PASS	PASS	PASS	

East passes, and South opens 1♥. With only 11 high-card points, North doesn't have enough for a 2/1 game-forcing response. Instead, North starts with a forcing 1NT.

South rebids 2♥ to show the six-card suit. With 11 points, North has enough to invite game, even though opener has shown a minimum-strength opening bid hand. North now knows the partnership has an eight-card heart fit and can invite game by raising to 3♥. With 13 high-card points plus 2 length points for the six-card suit, South has enough extra to accept the invitation and continue to 4♥.

Suggested Opening Lead

West would lead the ♣A, top of the broken sequence in one of the unbid suits.

Suggested Play

Declarer has three spade tricks to go with the ♥A and ♦A-K. That's six tricks. So South needs four more tricks from the heart suit. That should be easy enough if the missing hearts are divided 3-2. Declarer can afford to lose a heart trick to the defenders' ♥K.

Since declarer can afford to lose one heart trick but not two, declarer should start by leading the ♥A, followed by another heart. On the actual deal, East's ♥K falls under the ♥A. Declarer can then take the ♥Q and ♥J, losing only one heart trick to West's ♥10. Declarer would also lose only one heart trick if West held the singleton ♥K, or if the missing hearts were divided 3-2.

The danger of leading the ♥Q, planning to take a finesse, can be seen in the actual layout[46]. The finesse loses to East's ♥K, and declarer has to lose a second heart trick to West's ♥10. Playing the ♥A first gives declarer the best chance of losing only one heart trick.

Suggested Defense

The defenders get only one club trick, but will eventually get a diamond trick as well. If declarer starts the heart suit by leading the ♥Q or ♥J, the defenders will also get two heart tricks to defeat the contract.

Conclusion

The forcing 1NT response to 1♥ or 1♠ has a wide range of about 6–12 points. With the top of the range, responder plans to bid again, inviting game, even when opener shows a minimum hand of about 13–16 points.

---

[46] The result would be the same if the East-West hearts were exchanged. When South leads the ♥Q, West plays the ♥K, and dummy would win the ♥A. Declarer could take the ♥J, but would have to lose two tricks to East's ♥10-9.

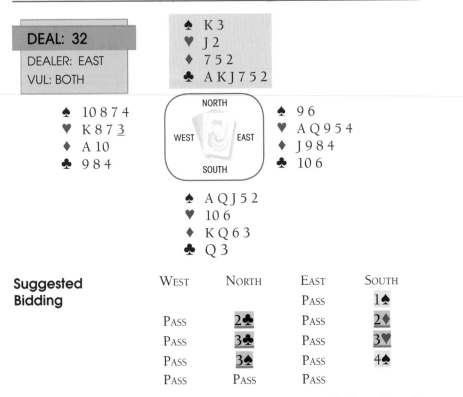

	WEST	NORTH	EAST	SOUTH
			PASS	1♠
	PASS	2♣	PASS	2♦
	PASS	3♣	PASS	3♥
	PASS	3♠	PASS	4♠
	PASS	PASS	PASS	

Suggested Bidding

East passes. South opens 1♠, North makes a 2/1 response of 2♣, and South shows the second suit with a 2♦ rebid. North can now rebid the clubs to show the extra length without any fear of being passed below game.

Over North's 3♣, South has to decide what to do next. Rebidding spades would show a six-card suit; rebidding diamonds would show a five-card suit; raising clubs would take the partnership beyond 3NT; and bidding 3NT would tend to show a stopper in hearts. So South bids 3♥, the fourth suit. The bid of the fourth suit is artificial, saying nothing about hearts. With a good holding in hearts, South could bid 3NT. Unless the 3♥ bid is a control-showing bid, which South would clarify later, it says, "I'm not sure WHERE we belong."

With nothing in hearts, North shows some help in spades. With three-card support, North would have raised spades earlier. South knows partner doesn't have three spades, but can't bid notrump with nothing in hearts. So South settles for game in spades. Another possibility might be game in clubs, but 4♠ requires only ten tricks.

Suggested Opening Lead

The opponents' reluctance to bid notrump makes a heart lead stand out. South's 3♥ bid doesn't necessarily show hearts. So West will lead the ♥3, fourth highest.

Suggested Play

The defenders can take the first two heart tricks and the ♦A, but then have to give declarer the lead. Declarer can draw all the outstanding trumps, and then take the club winners. Declarer finishes with ten tricks.

Suggested Defense

Against four spades, the defenders cannot do better than take two hearts and the ♦A. In fact, if they don't take their tricks, declarer can make an overtrick, taking five spade tricks and six club tricks.

If North-South play in 3NT, a heart lead from either side will let the defenders take the first five heart tricks and the ♦A to defeat the contract two tricks. If North becomes declarer in 5♣, the defenders can take two heart tricks and the ♦A to defeat the contract.

Conclusion

In standard bidding, North and South are likely to play in 3NT:

West	North	East	South
			1♠
Pass	2♣	Pass	2♦
Pass	3NT?	Pass	Pass
Pass			

North has a difficult choice after opener's 2♦ rebid. With enough for game, North can't afford to rebid only 3♣, which might be passed. A jump to 4♣, which would be forcing, takes the partnership past 3NT, and on this deal would get the partnership to 5♣, down one[47].

Using 2/1, the partnership can take its time to explore for the best contract. It takes some good judgment to land in 4♠, but the partnership has the tools to do it.

---

[47] North might choose 2♥, fourth suit forcing, rather than 3NT, and the partnership might also land in the 5-2 spade fit. However, the partnership is likely to be on much shakier ground than after the 2/1 game-forcing start.

Do not fear to be eccentric in opinion, for every opinion now accepted was once eccentric.

—BERTRAND RUSSELL, (1872–1970)

Appendices

Appendix 1—2/1 Versus Fourth Suit Forcing

One advantage of 2/1 Game Force is that responder no longer has to worry about finding a forcing rebid, since any rebid below game is forcing. In standard methods, many of responder's rebids are not forcing, such as 2NT, a rebid of responder's suit, or a raise of opener's suit. With 13 or more points, therefore, responder must either jump right to game or find another forcing bid such as a new suit or a jump in an old suit. A bid of the fourth suit by responder is often used as an artificial game force in standard bidding. Could this be used instead of 2/1 Game Force?

Sometimes, fourth suit forcing works equally well. For example:

OPENER	RESPONDER
♠ K J 7 5 3	♠ Q 2
♥ A K 10 7 2	♥ Q 8 3
♦ 8 4	♦ A J 3
♣ 6	♣ A 10 9 5 4

The standard auction would begin:

OPENER	RESPONDER
1♠	2♣
2♥	?

Unsure of the best contract, responder could make an artificial fourth suit bid of 3♦. This is a marathon bid, forcing to game. The auction would continue:

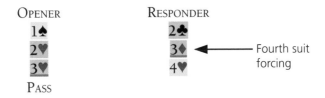

OPENER	RESPONDER	
1♠	2♣	
2♥	3♦	← Fourth suit forcing
3♥	4♥	
PASS		

Over the artificial game-forcing 3♦ bid, opener can rebid the five-card heart suit, and responder can place the partnership in the best contract. In 2/1 Game Force, responder would have made the descriptive rebid of 2NT, but both approaches would lead to the same result.

However, suppose we make a slight change to opener's hand:

Opener	Responder
♠ K J 7 5 3	♠ Q 2
♥ A K 7 2	♥ Q 8 3
♦ 10 4	♦ A J 3
♣ K 6	♣ A 10 9 5 4

In standard methods, using fourth suit forcing, the auction now begins:

Opener	Responder
1♠	2♣
2♥	3♦ ◄——— Fourth suit forcing
?	

What is opener to do at this point? Opener doesn't want to bid 3NT with nothing in diamonds, since responder's 3♦ was totally artificial. If opener gives a preference to 4♣, the partnership has missed its best spot of 3NT.

Using 2/1 Game Force, the auction goes:

Opener	Responder
1♠	2♣
2♥	2NT
3NT	Pass

Responder rebids a natural, forcing 2NT, and opener simply raises to 3NT with nothing further to say.

So while the use of fourth suit forcing does resolve some problems in standard bidding, it doesn't resolve all of them. 2/1 Game Force will usually make the auction more comfortable for the partnership. In addition, the bid of the fourth suit can be put to a slightly different purpose when playing 2/1 Game Force. See the discussion of fourth suit in the section on Responder's Rebid in Chapter 3.

Appendix 2 – Opener's Standard Rebids
After a 1NT Response

After an opening 1♥ or 1♠ and a 1NT response, opener's rebid is the same when playing 2/1 Game Force as in standard methods, with one exception. With a minimum balanced hand, opener can pass playing standard. Playing 2/1 Game Force, opener must bid again, since the 1NT response is forcing unless responder passed initially.

Here are opener's rebids after a 1♥ opening and a 1NT response:

	OPENER		RESPONDER
	1♥		1NT
	?		

REBID	STRENGTH	DESCRIPTION	NOTES
4♥	19–21	6+ hearts	
3♥	17–18	6+ hearts	
3♦	19–21	5+ hearts and 4+ diamonds	Jump shift.
3♣	19–21	5+ hearts and 4+ clubs	Jump shift.
2NT	18–19	Balanced	Opener would open 1NT with a balanced 15–17 and 2NT with 20–21.
2♠	17–21	5+ hearts and 4+ spades	Reverse.
2♥	13–16	6+ hearts	
2♦	13–18	5+ hearts and 4+ diamonds	
2♣	13–18	5+ hearts and 4+ clubs	
Pass	13-14	Balanced	Opener could not pass playing 1NT forcing.

WEST	NORTH	EAST	SOUTH
			1♥
PASS	1NT	PASS	?

NORTH
WEST · EAST
SOUTH

♠ 4
♥ A Q 8 6 3
♦ A K 10 5
♣ K 7 3

Rebid 2♦. Opener's rebid of a lower-ranking suit at the two level covers a wide range, 13-18 points: any hand not strong enough for a jump shift. Responder will usually give preference back to opener's first suit, giving opener an opportunity to show extra strength by bidding again.

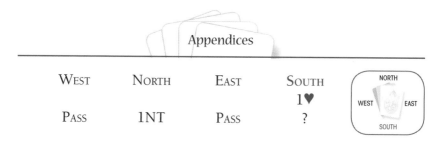

WEST	NORTH	EAST	SOUTH
			1♥
PASS	1NT	PASS	?

♠ K 4
♥ A K J 9 8 4
♦ A 8 5
♣ 7 3

Rebid 3♥. This hand is worth 15 high-card points plus 2 length points for the six-card suit. That's enough to make a jump rebid over the 1NT response. The jump isn't forcing, just highly invitational.

Opener's rebids after a 1♠ opening follow a similar pattern. The only difference is that opener has no reverse available.

OPENER	RESPONDER
1♠	1NT
?	

REBID	STRENGTH	DESCRIPTION	NOTES
4♠	19–21	6+ spades	
3♠	17–18	6+ spades	
3♥	19–21	5+ spades and 4+ hearts	Jump shift.
3♦	19–21	5+ spades and 4+ diamonds	Jump shift.
3♣	19–21	5+ spades and 4+ clubs	Jump shift.
2NT	18–19	Balanced	Opener would open 1NT with a balanced 15–17 and 2NT with 20–21.
2♠	13–16	6+ spades	
2♥	13–16	5+ spades and 4+ hearts	
2♦	13–18	5+ spades and 4+ diamonds	
2♣	13–18	5+ spades and 4+ clubs	
Pass	13–14	Balanced	Opener could not pass playing 1NT forcing.

Appendix 3 – Semi-Forcing 1NT

A disadvantage of the forcing 1NT response to 1♥ and 1♠, is that the partnership can never play in 1NT, even when it is the best contract. For example:

OPENER	RESPONDER
♠ A Q 10	♠ K 7 3
♥ J 9 7 6 2	♥ 4 3
♦ J 8	♦ K Q 10 5
♣ A 5 3	♣ 9 7 6 2

OPENER	RESPONDER
1♥	1NT
2♣	?

If responder passes 2♣, the partnership is in a 4-3 fit that is unlikely to make. If responder gives preference to 2♥, the partnership is in a contract that has no chance of taking eight tricks. The best spot is 1NT. Three tricks can be promoted in diamonds to go with three spade tricks and the ♣A.

Such occasional poor results are the price most partnerships are willing to accept for the overall advantages of the forcing 1NT. Some partnerships, however, prefer a slight variation:

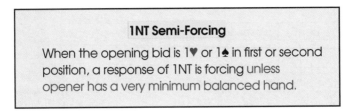

1NT Semi-Forcing

When the opening bid is 1♥ or 1♠ in first or second position, a response of 1NT is forcing unless opener has a very minimum balanced hand.

With this agreement, opener could pass the responder's 1NT bid in the above auction, and the partnership would stop in a makeable partscore.

The danger in this approach is that responder could have as many as 12 points, and could have a three-card limit raise of opener's major. So opener should only pass with an absolute minimum of 12 or 13 points, with a hand that would not have accepted a three-card invitational raise.

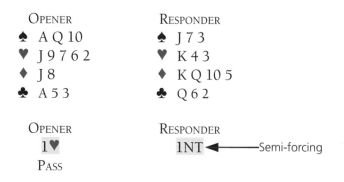

Opener	Responder
♠ A Q 10	♠ J 7 3
♥ J 9 7 6 2	♥ K 4 3
♦ J 8	♦ K Q 10 5
♣ A 5 3	♣ Q 6 2

Opener	Responder
1♥	1NT ◄——————Semi-forcing
Pass	

Here responder was planning to bid 3♥ over opener's rebid. When opener passes, the partnership plays in 1NT rather than 3♥, but that's okay since opener was going to pass 3♥. 1NT is actually a safer contract than 3♥.

Opener	Responder
♠ A Q 10	♠ J 7 3
♥ A Q 10 6 2	♥ K 4 3
♦ J 8 2	♦ K Q 10 5
♣ 5 3	♣ Q 6 2

Opener	Responder
1♥	1NT ◄——————Semi-forcing
2♦	3♥
4♥	Pass

Here opener has a good enough hand to accept an invitational raise, so opener bids over the semi-forcing 1NT. When responder invites game in hearts, opener accepts. Declarer will need the ♠K favorably placed, but 4♥ is a good contract.

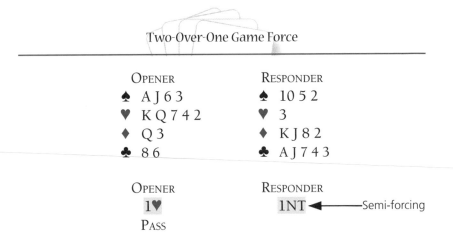

OPENER	RESPONDER
♠ A J 6 3	♠ 10 5 2
♥ K Q 7 4 2	♥ 3
♦ Q 3	♦ K J 8 2
♣ 8 6	♣ A J 7 4 3

OPENER	RESPONDER
1♥	1NT ◄——————Semi-forcing
PASS	

This is a particularly awkward hand for opener if the 1NT response is forcing. Opener has no three-card minor to bid, and is not strong enough to reverse into 2♠, especially since responder denied a four-card spade suit. Playing 1NT forcing, standard practice is to bid 2♣ on a doubleton in this situation, although some players might prefer 2♥. Playing 1NT semi-forcing, opener can simply pass.

Appendix 4 – 2/1 Challenges and Variations

One drawback of using 2/1 Game Force is that responder's 1NT has to cover a wide range of hands, all those with about 6-12 points that are not strong enough for a 2/1 response. After an opening bid of 1♥ or 1♠, the 1NT response is forcing, so responder will have another opportunity to describe the hand. However, a response of 1NT is not forcing over an opening bid of 1♦. That can be awkward when responder has an invitational hand with a good club suit:

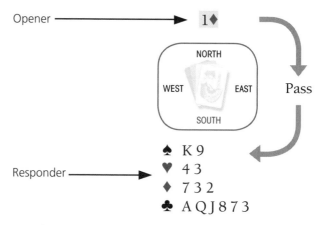

Opener   →   1♦   Pass

Responder   →
   ♠ K 9
   ♥ 4 3
   ♦ 7 3 2
   ♣ A Q J 8 7 3

With only 10 high-card points plus 2 length points for the six-card club suit, responder doesn't have quite enough for a game-forcing response of 2♣. A response of 1NT would show about 6-10 points, and might result in missing a game when opener has some extra strength, but not enough to move over 1NT. A jump to 2NT would be invitational, showing a balanced hand of about 11-12 points. That's probably what responder will have to bid with no alternative, but it is uncomfortable with an unbalanced hand and no stopper in hearts.

There are a couple of ways the partnership can address this problem.

2/1 GAME FORCE EXCEPT 2♣

Some partnerships play that a 2/1 response is game-forcing except for a response of 2♣. If responder bids 2♣ and then follows with 3♣, responder is showing only an invitational hand. Opener can pass. This handles the previous hand nicely.

With a good club suit and 13 or more points, however, responder has to find a rebid other than 3♣, to make sure opener does not pass. This loses the advantage of the 2/1 game-forcing 2♣ response in this situation.

This variation isn't recommended for most partnerships, since it adds complexity to the straightforward 2/1 Game Force approach.

INVITATIONAL JUMP RESPONSES AT THE THREE LEVEL

Another approach for handling responder's challenge with invitational hands is for the partnership to play that responder's jump to the three level in a lower-ranking suit shows an invitational hand of about 11-12 points with a good six-card or longer suit. Since clubs are lower-ranking than diamonds, responder would jump to 3♣ over 1♦ with the earlier hand.

A big advantage of this approach is that it can also be used when the opening bid is 1♥ or 1♠. Responder would make the same invitational jump to 3♣ with this hand. In addition, this can be used any time responder has a suit that is lower-ranking than opener's suit. This allows responder to differentiate between weak hands with a long suit and invitational hands with a long suit. Consider these two hands that responder might hold when opener bids 1♠:

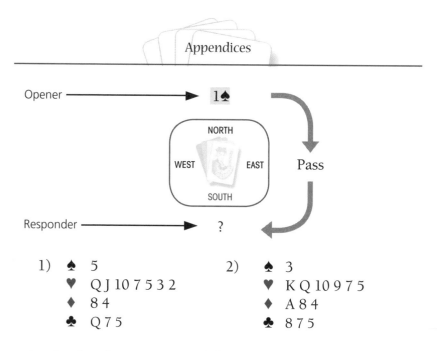

1) ♠ 5
   ♥ Q J 10 7 5 3 2
   ♦ 8 4
   ♣ Q 7 5

2) ♠ 3
   ♥ K Q 10 9 7 5
   ♦ A 8 4
   ♣ 8 7 5

Neither hand is strong enough for a game-forcing 2/1 response of 2♥. Suppose responder starts with a forcing 1NT response. There is not much problem if opener rebids 2♦. With the first hand, responder can bid 2♥, showing a weak hand with a long suit. With the second hand, responder can jump to 3♥, showing an invitational hand of about 11-12 points with a good heart suit.

However, what if opener rebids 2♠? Responder would like to sign off in 3♥ with the first hand, but make an invitational move to 3♥ with the second. Unfortunately, opener won't know which hand the 3♥ bid shows. Playing invitational jump responses, responder would start with a forcing 1NT with the first hand, and a subsequent heart bid would be limited to 6-10 points. With the second hand, responder would make an immediate jump to 3♥.

A downside to this approach is that it gives up the strong jump shift to the three level—although this is not particularly useful if the partnership uses 2/1—and it also gives up other uses for jumps to the three level, such as Bergen raises.

Appendix 5—Inverted Minor Suit Raises

When the opening bid is 1♣ or 1♦, responder usually has a comfortable time finding a response. With an unbalanced hand, responder can bid a new suit. With a balanced hand, responder can bid 1NT to show 6–10 points, 2NT to show 11–12, and 3NT to show 13–15. However, responder might be faced with an awkward choice with 13 or more points and good support for opener's minor.

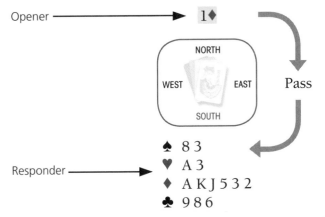

With an unbalanced hand and no stopper in either spades or clubs, the hand is unsuitable for a jump to 3NT. A jump raise to 3♦ is invitational, and a response of 2♣ would tend to mislead partner about both the quality of the clubs and the diamond support. In standard methods, there is no easy way for responder to show a forcing raise of opener's minor.

A popular idea is to 'invert' the meaning of raises of opener's minor:

- A single raise is forcing, showing 11 or more points.
- A jump raise is weak, showing about 6–10 points.

Playing inverted minor suit raises, responder would raise to 2♦, forcing, with the above hand, and then continue to at least game.

The partnership still needs to discuss how to differentiate between invitational raises of 11-12 points and forcing raises of 13 or more[48], but this approach helps with hands like the one above.

---

[48] Most partnerships agree that the auction can stop in 2NT or three of the minor suit when responder has 11–12 points. Any further bidding by responder shows 13 or more points.

Appendix 6 – Drury

Suppose opener bids 1♠ and responder has this hand:

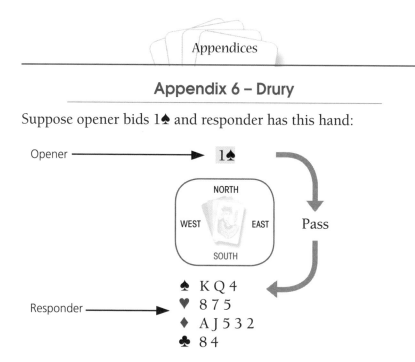

Opener ──────────────────→ 1♠

Pass

Responder ──────────────→
♠ K Q 4
♥ 8 7 5
♦ A J 5 3 2
♣ 8 4

Responder has 10 high-card points, and with three-card support for spades, can add a dummy point for the doubleton club. To show a three-card invitational raise, responder would start with a forcing 1NT response and then bid 3♠ over opener's rebid. However, suppose responder passed initially:

OPENER	RESPONDER
	PASS
1♠	?

A response of 1NT is no longer forcing when responder is a passed hand. A response of 2♦ is also non-forcing. Opener could pass with a minimum hand. Responder could jump to 3♠, but that tends to show four-card support, and it might get the partnership too high if opener has a 'light' opening bid—a common tactic when opener is in third or fourth position.

To resolve this dilemma, many partnerships use the Drury convention:

DRURY

When partner opens 1♥ or 1♠ in third or fourth position, a response of 2♣ is artificial, showing three-card or longer support and interest in game.

Opener's standard reply to Drury is to bid 2♦ with no interest in game, but most players use Reverse Drury:

OPENER'S REBID - REVERSE DRURY

After the 2♣ Drury inquiry, opener rebids the major suit with no interest in game.

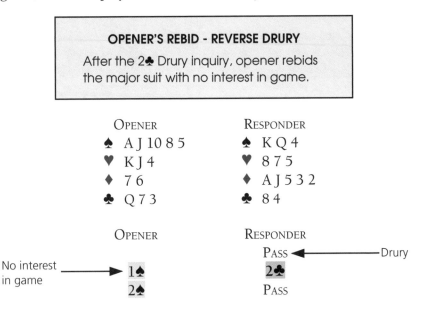

OPENER	RESPONDER
♠ A J 10 8 5	♠ K Q 4
♥ K J 4	♥ 8 7 5
♦ 7 6	♦ A J 5 3 2
♣ Q 7 3	♣ 8 4

OPENER	RESPONDER
	PASS ◄——————— Drury
No interest in game ——► 1♠	2♣
2♠	PASS

After responder passes, opener opens 1♠ with only 11 high-card points and 1 length point for the fifth spade. Responder uses the artificial Drury 2♣ response to show support for opener's major and interest in reaching game. With a sub-standard opening and no interest in game, opener simply returns to the agreed trump suit and responder accepts opener's decision to play in partscore. The partnership avoids getting to 3♠, which is likely to be too high.

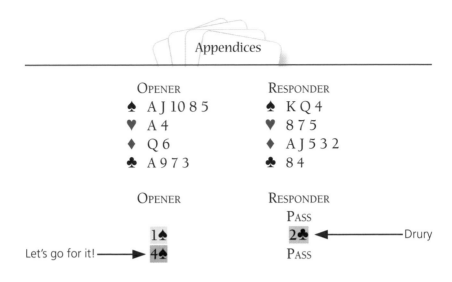

OPENER	RESPONDER
♠ A J 10 8 5	♠ K Q 4
♥ A 4	♥ 8 7 5
♦ Q 6	♦ A J 5 3 2
♣ A 9 7 3	♣ 8 4

OPENER	RESPONDER
	PASS
1♠	2♣ ◄──────── Drury
Let's go for it! ──► 4♠	PASS

Here opener has enough extra strength to accept the game invitation. There are other possible continuations after the 2♣ bid, but this is the basic idea.

Appendix 7—Jump Rebids After 2/1

Since all bids below game are forcing after a 2/1 response and the focus is on finding WHERE to play, there is little reason for either opener or responder to use up extra bidding room by jumping a level. Nevertheless, experienced partnerships do assign specific meanings to jump rebids. There are typically two agreements:

- Opener's jump rebid of the original suit shows a solid, or semi-solid suit—a suit that has at most one loser even if partner has a singleton or void.
- A jump rebid in a new suit is a *splinter bid*—showing support for partner's suit and a singleton or void in the bid suit.

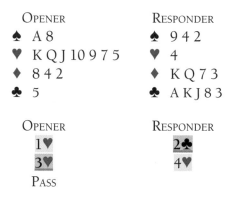

OPENER	RESPONDER
♠ A 8	♠ 9 4 2
♥ K Q J 10 9 7 5	♥ 4
♦ 8 4 2	♦ K Q 7 3
♣ 5	♣ A K J 8 3

OPENER	RESPONDER
1♥	2♣
3♥	4♥
PASS	

After the 2♣ response, opener can show the solid heart suit with a jump rebid of 3♥ rather than the usual rebid of 2♥. Opener doesn't need any extra strength for the jump, just a suit with at most one loser. Here opener has seven playing tricks with hearts as trumps. Responder has no concern about raising to 4♥ with a singleton heart. Responder knows that the partnership won't lose more than one heart trick.

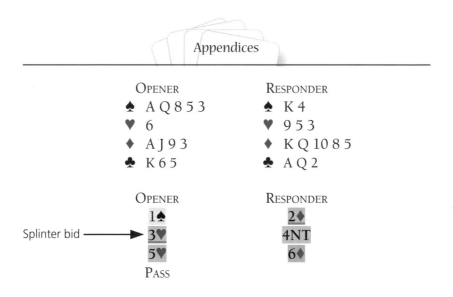

	OPENER	RESPONDER
♠	A Q 8 5 3	♠ K 4
♥	6	♥ 9 5 3
♦	A J 9 3	♦ K Q 10 8 5
♣	K 6 5	♣ A Q 2

	OPENER	RESPONDER
	1♠	2♦
Splinter bid ⟶	3♥	4NT
	5♥	6♦
	PASS	

When responder bids 2♦, opener has an excellent fit for diamonds and a singleton heart. If the partnership is familiar with splinter bids, opener can describe the hand nicely with a jump to 3♥. There's no need for this to be used to show a strong hand with hearts, since opener could simply rebid 2♥ to show hearts, planning to show the extra strength later. That's one of the advantages of playing 2/1 Game Force. Once responder knows there is a good diamond fit and at most one heart loser—since responder's remaining hearts can be trumped in opener's hand—that's enough to launch into Blackwood and bid a slam when opener shows two aces.

Splinter bids are a valuable tool for reaching good slams with fewer than the usual number of high-card points. Here the partnership has only 28 combined high-card points. However, valuing holdings opposite shortness in partner's hand requires some experience.

Appendix 8 – Blackwood and Key Card Blackwood

BLACKWOOD

Once a trump suit has been agreed, a bid of 4NT asks how many aces partner holds. In standard Blackwood, partner responds:

5♠	Three aces
5♥	Two aces
5♦	One ace
5♣	Zero or all four aces

If the partnership is missing two aces, it can stop at the five level in the agreed trump suit. If only one ace is missing, a small slam can be bid in the agreed trump suit. If the partnership holds all the aces and there is the possibility of a grand slam, a subsequent bid of 5NT asks about kings. The responses are:

6NT	Four kings
6♠	Three kings
6♥	Two kings
6♦	One king
6♣	Zero kings

KEY CARD BLACKWOOD

Once the trump suit is decided and the partnership is considering a slam, the focus turns to controls. To bid a small slam, the partnership wants some assurance that the defenders won't take the first two tricks. Control-showing, combined with Blackwood, helps resolve this issue. However, there are other key cards in a trump slam. While declarer may be able to get around a missing king in a side suit—by trumping the losers or discarding them—there's no getting around the trump king. It's a key card. The trump queen will also be a valuable card to hold.

Standard Blackwood doesn't deal with the trump king, and control-showing bids don't deal with the trump suit at all. So many partnerships prefer a variation of Blackwood that does take these cards into account.

In these variations, there are five key cards—the four aces and the trump king—to be taken into consideration, along with the trump queen, when responding to 4NT. This means that the responses to 4NT must be changed to accommodate the additional possibilities.

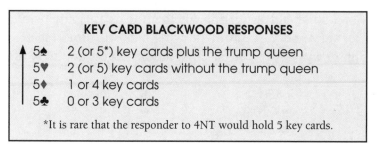

KEY CARD BLACKWOOD RESPONSES

5♠ 2 (or 5*) key cards plus the trump queen
5♥ 2 (or 5) key cards without the trump queen
5♦ 1 or 4 key cards
5♣ 0 or 3 key cards

*It is rare that the responder to 4NT would hold 5 key cards.

Some partnerships prefer to reverse the meaning of the 5♣ and 5♦ responses.

If the response is 5♣ or 5♦, the next suit that is not trump asks about the trump queen. Without the queen, partner returns to the agreed trump suit. With the trump queen, partner bids the cheapest outside suit that has a king, or jumps in the trump suit with no outside king.

A subsequent bid of 5NT asks partner to show a king outside the trump suit. With more than one king, partner bids kings 'up the line', cheapest first[49]. With no king, partner returns to the agreed trump suit at the six level.

Since key card responses to Blackwood add some complexity, especially with continuations to ask about the trump queen or outside kings, the partnership should discuss this thoroughly before changing from standard responses.

---

[49] Some partnerships use other variations.

Appendix 9—Additional Considerations in Showing Controls

HAS THE TRUMP SUIT BEEN AGREED?

After a 2/1 response, when either player raises partner's major suit, the trump suit is set and the partnership can focus on How HIGH: Game or Slam? When a minor suit is raised, however, there is still the possibility that the partnership may want to play in 3NT. So bids below 3NT after a minor suit has been raised carry some ambiguity. They may still be investigating whether the partnership belongs in 3NT, or they may be control-showing bids with interest in slam. The intent will have to be clarified on the next round of bidding.

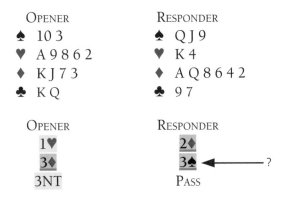

OPENER	RESPONDER
♠ 10 3	♠ Q J 9
♥ A 9 8 6 2	♥ K 4
♦ K J 7 3	♦ A Q 8 6 4 2
♣ K Q	♣ 9 7

OPENER	RESPONDER
1♥	2♦
3♦	3♠ ← ?
3NT	PASS

After opener raises responder's diamonds, responder still isn't certain WHERE the partnership belongs. Responder doesn't want to bid 3NT with no stopper in clubs, so responder shows some values in spades, hoping opener can bid 3NT. Since the partnership is still below 3NT, opener should assume this is a try for the best game, not a slam try, and bid 3NT with a club stopper. 3NT is an excellent contract. 5♦ has three top losers, the ♠A-K and ♣A.

What if responder is interested in getting to slam?

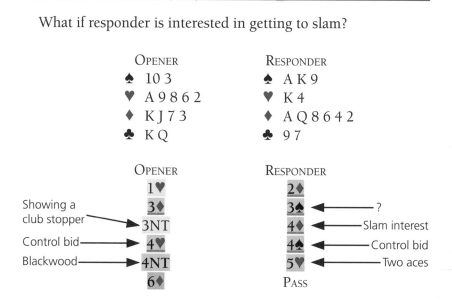

OPENER	RESPONDER
♠ 10 3	♠ A K 9
♥ A 9 8 6 2	♥ K 4
♦ K J 7 3	♦ A Q 8 6 4 2
♣ K Q	♣ 9 7

	OPENER		RESPONDER	
	1♥		2♦	
Showing a club stopper	3♦		3♠ ←	?
	3NT		4♦ ←	Slam interest
Control bid →	4♥		4♠ ←	Control bid
Blackwood →	4NT		5♥ ←	Two aces
	6♦		PASS	

Here responder wants to go for a slam once opener raises diamonds, but can't afford to bid Blackwood with two low clubs. If opener shows one ace—as on the actual deal—responder still won't know whether the opponents can take the first two club tricks. So responder bids 3♠ to start the control-showing process.

Opener isn't sure whether the 3♠ bid is a diamond slam try or looking to play in 3NT rather than 5♦. For now, opener assumes responder is still looking to play in notrump, and holding a club stopper, bids 3NT.

Now responder clarifies the situation by bidding 4♦, since responder would have passed the 3NT bid if that was where responder was looking to play. So the 4♦ bid says, "My previous 3♠ was a control-showing bid. Now I'm interested in slam."

Opener now gets the message and cooperates by showing the ♥A. Responder's 4♠ bid shows second-round control of spades, the ♠K, since the 3♠ bid showed first-round control. Assured by the club holding that the partnership has at least first- or second-round control in all suits, opener can now simplify proceedings by bidding Blackwood. Responder shows two aces, and opener bids the slam.

SHOWING CONTROLS BEYOND GAME

Although it is rare to go past game when showing controls, there are exceptions:

- Holding what is likely to be a key control, but not enough extra strength to assume the captaincy.
- Holding enough strength for slam, but two low cards in a suit in which partner may hold a control.

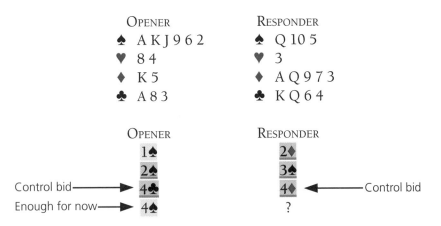

OPENER	RESPONDER
♠ A K J 9 6 2	♠ Q 10 5
♥ 8 4	♥ 3
♦ K 5	♦ A Q 9 7 3
♣ A 8 3	♣ K Q 6 4

	OPENER	RESPONDER	
	1♠	2♦	
	2♠	3♠	
Control bid —→	4♣	4♦	←— Control bid
Enough for now —→	4♠	?	

Responder's raise to 3♠ sets the trump suit, and opener shows interest in slam with a control bid of 4♣. Responder cooperates by bidding 4♦. Opener is still worried about the heart suit and simply returns to the agreed trump suit.

Responder can infer that opener is probably concerned about a control in hearts. Responder has some extra values, but not enough to take command and bid Blackwood. Responder doesn't know that opener has the valuable ♦K, for example. To show some further interest in slam, responder can make another move by showing the control in hearts.

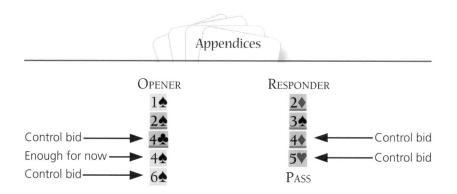

This brings opener back to life. When responder shows a control in hearts, opener has enough to take the partnership to 6♠.

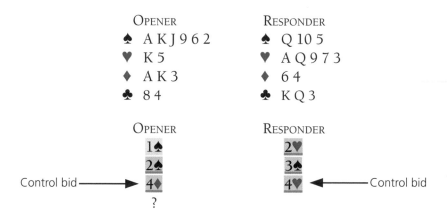

Here opener has enough to go for slam once spades are agreed, but doesn't want to immediately jump to Blackwood without a control in the club suit. Instead, opener starts a control-showing sequence with 4♦, and responder cooperates by bidding 4♥. Opener is still worried about clubs, but has too much to give up on slam. Blackwood still won't resolve the problem in clubs, so opener can try another control-showing bid, even though it takes the partnership beyond game.

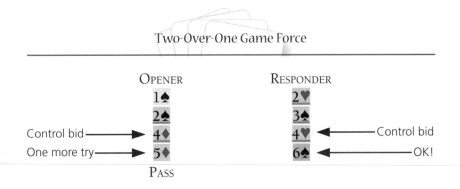

	OPENER	RESPONDER	
	1♠	2♥	
	2♠	3♠	
Control bid ——→	4♦	4♥	←—— Control bid
One more try ——→	5♦	6♠	←—— OK!
	PASS		

It is now obvious to responder that opener is concerned about clubs. Opener has bypassed the club suit twice, denying either first- or second-round control in clubs. Holding second-round control in clubs, responder can recognize that this is what opener needs and bids the slam. Without a control in clubs, responder would simply return to 5♠.

Going beyond game would be risky if opener held three low clubs, since the defenders might take the first three tricks, even if the partnership stops at the five level. In such situations, it is usually best to simply bid game and leave any further move up to partner. When in doubt, take the plus score!

Glossary

1NT Forcing—Conventional agreement that when opener bids 1♥ or 1♠ in first or second position, and the next player passes, a response of 1NT shows about 6-12 points and is forcing. (page 36)

1NT Semi-forcing—Conventional agreement that when opener bids 1♥ or 1♠ in first or second position, and the next player passes, a response of 1NT shows about 6-12 points and is forcing, unless opener has a minimum balanced hand. (page 216)

Blackwood Convention—A bid of 4NT after a trump suit has been agreed to ask for the number of aces held by partner. The responses are: 5♣, 0 or 4; 5♦, 1; 5♥, 2; 5♠, 3. It is used when the partnership has enough combined strength for a slam contract, but wants to check that it isn't missing too many aces. If the partnership is interested in a grand slam, a subsequent bid of 5NT asks for the number of kings held by partner. (page 133)

Blocked—A suit in which the winners cannot be taken immediately because of entry problems. (page 95, 121)

Control—A holding in a suit which prevents the opponents from immediately taking one or two tricks. The partnership can find out about controls through Blackwood or control-showing bids. (page 14, 139)

Control-showing Bid—A bid that shows first- or second-round control in the suit bid. (page 15, 139)

Cooperative Double—A double that shows values, and leaves the decision to partner whether to pass for penalty or bid further. (page 107)

Crossruff—A play technique in which cards are ruffed in both the partnership's hands, thus using the trumps separately. (page 117, 207)

Cuebid—The bid of a suit already bid by the opponents. This is typically used as an artificial forcing bid in many competitive situations. It is sometimes used as another term for a control-showing bid. (page 14)

Dangerous Opponent—An opponent that declarer does not want to gain the lead. The opponent may have winners to take or be in position to make a damaging lead that could defeat the contract. (page 121)

Drury—An artificial 2♣ response to an opening bid of 1♥ or 1♠ in third or fourth position showing support for opener's major and interest in reaching game. In standard Drury, a rebid of 2♦ by opener shows no interest in game; in reverse Drury, a rebid of the major shows no interest in game. (page 63, 223)

Dummy Points—The valuation of shortness in a hand that is likely to be the dummy after a trump fit has been found: void, 5 points; singleton, 3 points; doubleton, 1 point. (page 129)

False Preference—Responder's return to opener's first bid suit when holding more cards in opener's second suit. (page 44)

Fast Arrival—The principle that bidding quickly to a contract shows no interest in going any higher. Conversely, bidding slowly toward the contract shows interest in bidding more. (page 164)

First-Round Control—A holding that prevents the opponents from taking the first trick in a suit: the ace, or a void in a suit contract. (page 132)

Forcing Bid—A bid that partner is not expected to pass. (page 4)

Forcing 1NT—Conventional agreement that when opener bids 1♥ or 1♠ in first or second position, and the next player passes, a response of 1NT shows about 6-12 points and is forcing. (page 36)

Fourth Suit Forcing—An agreement that a bid of the fourth suit is artificial and forcing; usually played as forcing to game. (page 211)

High Card Points (HCPs)—The value of high cards in a hand: ace, 4; king, 3; queen, 2; jack, 1. (page 7)

How High—The level at which the contract should be played.

Inverted Minor Suit Raises—A conventional agreement that a single raise of opener's minor suit is forcing for one round, showing about 11 or more points, while a jump raise is non-forcing and shows a weaker hand, about 6-10 points. Essentially, the meaning of raises to the two level and the three level are reversed from standard practice. (page 222)

Invitational Bid—A bid which encourages partner to continue bidding, but allows partner to pass with minimum values for what has been promised so far. (page 4)

Jump Shift—A jump one level higher than necessary in a new suit. (page 5)

Key Card Blackwood—A variation of Blackwood that includes the trump king and queen in the responses. (page 228)

Length Points—The valuation assigned to long suits in a hand: five-card suit, 1 point; six-card suit, 2 points; seven-card suit, 3 points; eight-card suit, 4 points. (page 7)

Light Opening—An opening bid with less strength than would typically be expected. This is a common tactic in third or fourth position. (page 18)

Loser on a Loser—Discarding a card that must be lost on a losing trick in another suit. This technique can be useful in many situations. (page 171, 191)

Marathon Bid—A bid that is forcing to at least a game contract. (page 5)

Old Suit—A suit previously bid by the partnership. (page 101)

Preference—Returning to the first suit that partner bid is called giving simple preference. (page 37)

Principle of Fast Arrival—The principle that bidding quickly to a contract shows no interest in going any higher. Conversely, bidding slowly toward the contract shows interest in bidding more. (page 164)

Quantitative Bid—A natural, non-forcing bid that limits the strength of the hand to a narrow range. After a 1NT opening, a raise to 4NT is quantitative, showing about 16-17 points. Opener can pass or bid on. (page 103)

Reverse (by Opener)—A rebid by opener in a new suit that prevents responder from returning to opener's original suit at the two level. (page 31)

Reverse Drury—A variation of Drury in which opener rebids the major suit over the 2♣ inquiry to show no interest in game. (page 224)

Safety Play—The play of a specific suit combination to cope with an unfavorable break. Also, any play which reduces or eliminates the risk of being defeated in the contract, even at the sacrifice of an overtrick. (page 75)

Second-Round Control—A holding that prevents the opponents from taking the first two tricks in a suit: the king, or a singleton in a suit contract. (page 132)

Semi-forcing 1NT— Conventional agreement that when opener bids 1♥ or 1♠ in first or second position, and the next player passes, a response of 1NT shows about 6-12 points and is forcing, unless opener has a minimum balanced hand. (page 216)

Signoff (Bid)—A bid that asks partner to pass. (page 3)

Splinter Bid—A conventional double jump in a new suit to show a fit with partner and a singleton or a void in the suit bid. (page 226)

Stopper—A holding in a suit that is likely to prevent the opponents from taking all the tricks in the suit. (page 95)

Temporizing Bid—A bid aimed at getting further information from partner with no real intention of playing in the bid suit. Typically made in a minor suit. (page 9)

Two-Over-One Game Force—A bidding approach in which a simple new suit response at the two level is forcing to at least game, after partner opens one of a suit in first or second position. (page 1)

Up the Line—Making the cheapest available bid with a choice of two or more suits to bid. (page 116, 144)

Where—The denomination (clubs, diamonds, hearts, spades, or notrump) in which the contract should be played.

Other publications by Audrey Grant with Baron Barclay

Bridge Basics Series

Bridge Basics 1 — An Introduction

Bridge Basics 2 — Competitive Bidding

Bridge Basics 3 — Popular Conventions

The Improving Your Judgment Series

Opening the Bidding

Doubles

Bridge At-A-Glance Companion Guide

Audrey Grant
www.AudreyGrant.com

I'd like to invite you to subscribe to *Better Bridge*, a bi-monthly, 24 page magazine for everyone who loves the game of bridge. Whether you play at home, at the club or in tournaments, you will find the *Better Bridge* magazine to be timely, insightful and thoroughly enjoyable. Each issue is full of useful information brought to you by the world's best players and writers; the up-to-date tips will have you playing better bridge!

AUDREY GRANT'S Better Bridge
• A magazine for all bridge players •

$29/YEAR U.S.
for 6 issues
SAVE $13 OFF THE SINGLE ISSUE PRICE

Audrey Grant's
BETTER BRIDGE

September/October 2004
Volume 9, Number 1

Articles that Keep You Up-to-date and Help Advance Your Game

Tips from Leading Experts

A Good Balance of Practical Advice on Bidding, Play, and Defense

Information on Where to Play: Clubs, Tournaments and Bridge Holidays

Published by Baron Barclay

BARON BARCLAY BRIDGE SUPPLIES
3600 Chamberlain Lane, Suite 230
Louisville, KY 40241   FAX: 502-426-2044
www.baronbarclay.com

1-800-274-2221
TOLL FREE IN THE U.S. & CANADA

VISA   MasterCard   NOVUS

BARON
BARCLAY
BRIDGE SUPPLY

Visit our web site to get
up-to-date information from Better Bridge.

www.BetterBridge.com OR www.AudreyGrant.com

PRODUCTS

Better Bridge material is prepared with the assistance of the Better Bridge Panel of world-wide experts and is available through books, disks, videos, magazines, and the Internet.

BRIDGE TEACHERS

Join the Better Bridge Teachers' Group if you are involved in bridge education. Teacher's manuals are available to assist in presenting bridge lessons to students.

CRUISES

Travel by ship, add Bridge at Sea, and you have a magic fit. Audrey Grant and the Better Bridge Team conduct bridge cruises to locations around the world.

FESTIVALS

Workshops and festivals are held in fine hotels and resorts across North America. Come with or without a partner . . . let us get a fourth for bridge.

BRIDGE QUIZ

Try the regularly updated quizzical pursuits. Test your bidding and play, spot the celebrities, and play detective at the table.

BRIDGE ONLINE

Playing bridge on the internet is becoming an increasingly popular pastime since you can play anywhere, anytime. Find out about the Audrey Grant bridge club and lessons.

CONTACT US

E-mail:	BetterBridge@BetterBridge.com
Phone:	1-888-266-4447
Fax:	1-416-322-6601
Write:	Better Bridge
	247 Wanless Avenue
	Toronto, ON M4N 1W5